"You're Perfect..."

and Other Lies Parents Tell

THE UGLY TRUTH ABOUT SPOILING YOUR KIDS

Loni Coombs

Published in Los Angeles, California, by Bird Street Books, Inc.

ISBN: 978-0-9854627-4-1

JACKET DESIGN: *the*BookDesigners
INTERIOR DESIGN: Maureen Forys, Happenstance Type-O-Rama

For my mother and father,
Carol Jean and Robert Holman Coombs,
the perfect parents for me.

Contents

Part 4
"What Do I Do When...?"

Part 5
Letting Go

Acknowledgments

I gratefully acknowledge: My mother and father, for their unconditional love and strength of moral character. My son, Trevor, who is my greatest blessing and the light of my life. My husband, Steve, for being a true partner and for making my world so fun. My brothers and sisters, Bob and Betzy, Kate, Karen and David, Holly and Chip, Krista, and David and Kim, for our unbreakable bond. And the rest of my wonderful family, Brittany, Chris, Courtney, Ryan, Westin, Trevor, and Kenzie, for sharing their lives with me. A special note of appreciation to Mom, Kate, and Luann, for their endless readings and critiques.

Welcome to the Real-Life School of Parenting

"You're perfect!" "You deserve first place, too!" "Don't you worry about that grade. That teacher has no idea what she is doing." "I'm sure it wasn't your fault. I'll take care of it." Do any of these parenting phrases sound familiar to you? Are you working hard to be a good parent, centering your life around your child and his or her every want and desire? If so, you may very well be headed for trouble and heartache. This is a perilous time for parents, and I know this firsthand.

For nearly two decades, I worked as a criminal prosecutor with the District Attorney's office in Los Angeles, prosecuting teenagers and young adults who had made some bad decisions, who had lost their way, and who were facing life-altering consequences. During that time, I also met an endless array of stunned parents in my courtroom who simply couldn't fathom what had happened. These parents gazed across the courtroom at their child standing next to their defense attorneys, facing the judge. As their bewilderment of shattered dreams and fear for an uncertain future grew, the parents would wonder, "How in the world did we end up here?" How in the world, they asked, did they end up *here*?

Those years spent working in the bowels of the grimy, gritty criminal justice system, thrust into the middle of countless catastrophic family meltdowns, revealed to me some very clear lessons for what parents can do—and *need* to do—to keep their children out of danger, not to mention handcuffs. My unique position and perspective, as well as my own experience being a mother and stepmother to my now-adult child and stepchildren, has afforded me specific insight into what works and what really doesn't.

I'm here to tell you that a lot of what you're doing is not working.

I have watched the direction of modern-day parenting take a dangerous turn. Hardworking, conscientious parents are desperately trying to give their children everything the parents didn't get when they were young. These parents think they're providing for their kids, even giving them a head start at life. They lavish their children with attention, opportunities, and material possessions. But there's an ugly truth about what these well-intentioned parents are doing to their children. Rather than giving them a head start, they're actually handicapping their kids and unwittingly creating a perilous "perfect storm" of trouble.

In essence, they are setting up an insidious mentality in their kids, instilling in them both an overwhelming *sense of entitlement* and a *lack of empathy for others*. The combination of these two factors can pave the way to completely ruin a child's life because it robs them of two crucial influences: the concept of rules and consequences and a concern for other people's feelings.

At best, children who grow up without these two guiding influences enter their 20s largely without any realistic idea about what it takes to succeed in life. They have a very weak work ethic, they seem more than willing to succumb to

"You're Perfect..." and Other Lies Parents Tell

self-destructive temptations, and they can't even see the paths that can lead them to true fulfillment and happiness.

Kids are growing up, hitting their 20s, and realizing one big, ugly truth—they're incapable of embracing adulthood and surviving and thriving in society.

You may be saying to yourself right now, "Hold on, Loni, *I'm* not raising *my child* like that!"

All I can say is, keep reading. Since the 1980s, parenting styles shifted to a more nurturing, more involved approach— perhaps too much nurturing and overbearing involvement. The children of these parents have and are growing up more "me-focused" than ever. Studies of teenagers and young adults today show a big increase in self-centeredness and narcissism. Some of the experts are referring to these kids as "Generation Me." More and more we are seeing teenagers and young adults commit egregious acts of callousness without any sense of responsibility for their actions or concern for their victims. Some of them are ending up in the criminal justice system.

And I'm talking about kids who are popular and intelligent— kids who can be very pleasant and never openly rebellious. They are children who have been raised by well-intentioned parents who genuinely thought they were doing the right thing. You could very well be one of those parents. That's why I've written this book.

"You're Perfect..." and Other Lies Parents Tell can benefit parents of children of any age: from toddlers all the way to young adults. It's for parents with children who, at the moment, think everything is okay, and it's for parents who are already worriedly crossing their fingers, hoping and praying that they don't get that collect call from the police station. It's a book that I believe will serve as a two-way mirror. Not only will you assess potential red flags in your child's life, but you'll discover valuable tools that you, as a parent, can use on a daily basis to keep

your child on the path to becoming a successful, productive citizen. I've designed this book to guide you as you teach your kids about building their "mental-moral core," instill in them such qualities as honesty and self-control, and ultimately give them a passion to strive for excellence. It will help you see for yourself the danger zones your kids are facing as well as assess your own parenting style. It will teach you how to *let go* at the right time and *allow* your kids to grow and develop their own confident, self-sufficient, empathetic identities.

Most importantly, I believe the principles and information in this book can keep you from ever having to experience that bleak, devastating moment when you realize that you've been caught up in your own false reality, thinking that your kids are perfect and that you can control everything that happens to them. The last thing I wish on any of you is that experience of driving to a courthouse for a harsh wake-up call—to learn that, in fact, your child is *not* perfect and you aren't actually in command of their world. At that moment, your mind will be flooded with questions and regret: Why didn't I see this coming? How could I have been so blind? So clueless?

Just to be clear, I have not written "one more child psychology" book. Although I have a bachelor's degree in psychology and I refer to current studies and research, I am not a child psychologist. What I focus on comes from my experiences and insights as a parent as well as a criminal prosecutor who has put far too many young people behind bars. I have had a unique view of hundreds of parents at their best and their worst. I've seen what works and what really does not—and you might be surprised by how much you're doing fits into the "what doesn't work" category.

The principles you're about to read are not complicated. But they require commitment and consistency. And as a parent, you're going to have to work. Believe me, in this day and age, you are destined to fail with your children if you resort to a kind of trial-and-error parenting style in which you basically hope and pray that what you are doing will result in your kids "turning out all right." Nor are you going to do your children any favors if you stick with some romantic delusion that you intuitively "know" how to parent based on how you were raised—either by doing just what your parents did (because they were so good) or by doing the exact opposite of what they did (because they were *not* so good). To raise happy and healthy children and to set them up for success, you need a whole new attitude. And I'm convinced that's exactly what you'll have by the time you read the last page of this book.

Yes, the earlier you apply this plan, the better. Still, it is *never* too late! Your children, no matter how old they are, can always benefit from these parenting techniques. And though I know you'll gain a deeper understanding of what's happening to you and your children if you start at the beginning of this book and read all the way through, let me suggest that if you're in crisis mode, then you should look first at the later chapters, which are full of immediate action plans to keep your child safe and prosperous.

The fact is that the way most parents are raising their children at this moment in history, despite their best intentions, might not result in happy, productive young adults. The ugly truth parents need to face is that telling your children that they are perfect and shielding them from the consequences of their actions while insisting that every child gets a first-place trophy is not good parenting. It is time to look at what you are really doing to your child and then find the courage to change.

Part 1

Generation Me:
What Is Happening
to My Kid?

1

Your Child Is at Risk and You Don't Even Know It

She entered the courtroom, looking like she had lost her way from the sandy Malibu beaches that shimmered mere steps away outside. With her messy blonde hair, sun-kissed complexion, and lanky limbs, I thought she could have been a cover model for *Glamour* magazine. But this 18-year-old girl wasn't dripping in diamonds and hip couture. Instead, her only adornment was an ill-fitting, blue, county-jail jumpsuit, accessorized with a pair of metal handcuffs.

I pulled her file from the pile stacked on the counsel's table in front of me. Her name was Sarah, and she was charged with possession of the drug ecstasy, with the intent to sell. The police report began with a familiar scenario, one that probably takes place every Friday night in towns across the country. Sarah had been a passenger in a car filled with her girlfriends, all dressed up for a night out on the town. With the music blasting and the girls chatting up a storm, it took a while for the driver to notice the sheriff's car flashing its lights behind her. When the deputy leaned toward the open window, he detected "an odor of what appeared to be marijuana emitting from the vehicle." All the occupants of the car were ordered out of the car and asked to show their driver's licenses. As Sarah was trying to retrieve her ID, a baggie of pills fell out of her sequined clutch. The deputy recovered the baggie from the ground and found enough ecstasy pills in it to arrest Sarah for intent to sell, a felony for which she was now facing three years in prison.

Sarah sat with all the other "custodies" waiting for their cases to be heard. She looked straight ahead, too petrified to glance at the toothless, transient woman on her right, who was charged with spitting on an officer and disturbing the peace. Nor did Sarah dare look in front of her, where sat an agitated ex-con who had been arrested, yet again, for beating his girlfriend. When her name was called, Sarah stood up, trying carefully not to disturb anyone. Her green eyes were filling rapidly with tears that she tried valiantly to fight back as she nodded to the judge's questions.

I noticed her glance out toward the audience portion of the courtroom when the judge asked if she would like to utilize the services of a public defender. I followed her sight line to a middle-aged couple sitting on the edge of their seats, straining to hear the judge's directions. The woman was clinging to the man's arm for support. Even across the crowded room I could see the family resemblance. And I could not help but immediately empathize with the feeling of helplessness as Sarah's parents tried to silently transmit all their love and concern across the room to their child.

Two hours later, I was sitting behind my desk, inviting Sarah's public defender as well as her mother and father to make themselves at home. The public defender introduced me to Dan and Julie, Sarah's parents. They sat down in the wobbly chairs I had pulled from the waiting room and tentatively asked if they could talk to me about Sarah. Observing their obvious anguish, I assented. The parents then took turns describing the wonderful daughter who was their only child and the light of their lives. They were certain the case against her was all a big mistake. The drugs must have been put in her purse by one of the other girls.

Not once did they ask me, "What did *we* do to get here?" Not once did they search their memories in an attempt to recall when or where they might have gotten off track raising their child. Still not grasping the harsh reality of the situation, they thought she might get a "do-over," without any admission of wrongdoing or imposition of consequence. They expected the criminal justice system to treat their daughter the same way they had treated her for her entire life.

During my years as a prosecutor, I observed some variation of this drama play out over and over again. It didn't matter if I was prosecuting gang cases, murder cases, drug cases, or burglary cases. It didn't matter if the defendants were rich kids, poor kids, celebrity kids, educated kids, or emotionally challenged kids. It was always the same tune, different verse. The kids were completely shocked that a judge was actually telling them that their behavior was unacceptable and that they were going to have to pay very real (and very scary) consequences. Meanwhile, the parents were just as shocked as their children. Sure, they'd say, they knew that their kids had made some mistakes, but deep down, they were certain nothing bad could ever really happen to their child.

■ Are Kids Today Really That Different?

Trust me, I'm not naïve. I know that it's a rite of passage for kids to get into some amount of trouble. Drinking, drug use, premature sexual activity, challenging authority, trying to push boundaries—it happens in every generation.

So, you ask, am I saying kids today are really that different from kids of the past? The answer is an emphatic "yes!"

Here's the deal: Your children live in one crazy, pumped-up, extreme world where temptation comes faster and from more sources than ever before. Challenges that used to arise in high school are now hitting our kids in middle school and even elementary school. And there are all the new struggles we couldn't even fathom when we were growing up—peer bullying, online predators, high-school shootings, the greater potency of such drugs such as marijuana and methamphetamines, homegrown methods to get high, extreme teen drinking, and gangs recruiting members in elementary school.

When you look at just about any study regarding juvenile life, you cannot do anything but conclude that our young people are in more jeopardy than ever before. Not convinced? Here's some data:

- Pot use among U.S. teens is on a dramatic rise. A study released in 2012 reported that nearly one in ten teens said they smoke marijuana at least twenty or more times a month.

- By the end of high school, almost three-quarters of the students have consumed alcohol, with 57 percent reporting that they have been drunk at least once. As for middle-school kids, 37 percent have tried alcohol by the eighth grade, with 17 percent reporting that they have been drunk at least once.

- Each day, nearly 4,000 kids under the age of 18 try their first cigarette, while *another* 1,000 become daily smokers.

- Nearly half of all high-school students, both boys and girls, report having had sexual intercourse.

- Young people, ages 13 to 29, accounted for 39 percent of all new HIV infections in 2009.

- Ten percent of 14- to 24-year-olds report having "sexted" a naked photo or video of themselves.

- One million children were harassed, threatened, or subjected to other forms of cyberbullying on Facebook during the past year.

Scary? Absolutely. Many experts are convinced that today's adolescents are more "at risk" than any other generation that has come before them. And I'm not referring only to kids who come from disadvantaged, lower-income environments. I'm talking about kids who, at this very moment, could be sitting on your sofa in your own home, watching your television, mindlessly clicking channels with the remote control.

And the issue here isn't only that our kids are not handling social temptations well. What's even more unsettling is that they don't seem to have much of a moral core to guide them in even the most basic of situations. In a study conducted in 2008 by education researchers, about 80 percent of high-school students reported *lying* to their parents about something significant, while 64 percent reported *cheating* in school. As for stealing, 30 percent of the students admitted they had shoplifted, and almost a quarter said they had stolen something from a family member. Here's the kicker: The students in that survey reported high self-appraisals of their character, with more than 90 percent saying they were satisfied with their ethics and character!

A lot of Generation Me kids think it's perfectly okay to look for "shortcuts" to get whatever they want. Seriously, we have a generation of kids who *lie, cheat, and steal*, and then brag about it on their social media network, and still think they are living good, moral lives!

■ The Rise of the Trophy Kid

It isn't hard to understand why this generation of teenagers is often referred to as Generation Me. They've grown up in an overscheduled environment where everything was planned for them and then essentially done for them. They've been handed trophies, not for winning but for simply showing up. Along the way, they've learned that the only purpose for money is to spend it on everything from the newest cell phones to the trendiest cars. So what if they cross the line, break the rules, and get in trouble? No problem. They know their parents will come to their rescue and bail them out.

In other words, they feel a sense of entitlement. They feel they deserve happiness, regardless of what they have or haven't done. They presume that certain gifts, accolades, or material wealth are "due" to them. Many of them have never been taught the concept of working hard to get what they want. They don't quite get that it takes time to obtain things of value. As a result, it never occurs to them to come up with any kind of life plan for what they are going to do with themselves. They simply roll their eyes whenever you try to talk to them about the future. They go through their days living under the delusion that the future will be handed to them on a silver platter the moment they snap their fingers.

And when you think about it, why shouldn't they? When so many of today's "trophy kids" are told from infancy by indulgent parents that they are beautiful and exceptional and that they can have anything they desire, the logical outcome is a generation that believes all of these things should continue for the rest of their life because Mommy and Daddy said it was so. The concept of delayed gratification makes no sense to them whatsoever.

True, since the dawn of time, young people have been consumed with themselves. That's the nature of being a kid. They are excessively concerned about their appearance and their standing within their immediate circle of friends. But, once again, the experts say that something is definitely different with this generation. Between 1982 and 2006, more than 16,000 high-school students were given the Narcissistic Personality Inventory, a test essentially indicating a person's level of narcissism, which is defined as an "inordinate fascination with oneself, excessive self-centeredness, self-preoccupation coupled with a lack of empathy for others; or self-absorption." In 1982, 35 percent of the students scored above average on the test. In 2006, the number of students with above-average scores jumped to more than 65 percent.

To me, it's entirely fitting that the members of Generation Me love using their cell phones to take "selfies" (photos of themselves) and post them on their Facebook pages. The Internet encourages kids to constantly promote themselves—and broadcast the minutiae of their lives—on blogs and through social media. I'm also not surprised that Generation Me loves reality television shows, which are essentially made-up dramas about made-up situations (the furthest thing from "reality" we can really get). For you, as parents, reality shows might seem like silly, harmless entertainment. And I certainly don't want to castigate the entire reality-show genre, because there are some shows that are indeed harmless (and, yes, a few of them can be somewhat enlightening). Unfortunately, the reality-show stars who seem to be the most popular with the younger demographic are either "characters" with great wealth, acting irresponsibly and frivolously, or "regular" people who end up with great wealth and fame by acting obnoxious, outrageous, rude, inappropriate, and extreme.

Kids who watch these shows are victims of what I call "toxic hero worship." They see these media-made pseudo-celebrities, who have had fame and fortune showered on them for getting drunk and falling down in bars, getting into screaming matches and tossing tables, or going to find a soul mate in front of 20 cameras, and they think, "So, that's what it means to be a success." For our teens, such behavior actually translates to a "get-rich-quick" mentality in which all you have to do is act obnoxious in front of cameras. And they learn very quickly what happens to nice, hardworking, mature "characters" on those shows. They get kicked off after the first season for being too "boring."

It's a mentality that flies in the face of the basic principles for humanity, such as working hard, taking responsibility, contributing to the betterment of society, or creating something of worth or beauty. On most reality TV shows, there is always that moment I call the "blubbering idiot" moment. It's the moment that, I'm sure, causes the show producers to rub their hands together with glee while I lower my head in shame for having wasted time and brain cells on such narcissistic drivel. It always involves a close-up camera shot of a contestant— maybe a woman looking for love on *The Bachelor* or a guy seeking fame on *American Idol* who has just been rejected. First comes a look of disbelief, a failure to comprehend, which then morphs into a rushed stream of the contestant mumbling, "What happened? I thought...I was perfect...how could this happen to me?" And then comes the ugly cry—the tears, the sobs, the turning away, but then coming back to question and cry some more.

Really? Forget that these contestants have been competing for only mere minutes or hours. Forget that the woman has had maybe one stilted conversation with the bachelor. Her heart has now been ripped out of her chest. Her future dreams have been destroyed. In her mind, she deserves him and all the fame and fortune and true love that would come with him. She wants it, and she wants it now! Being denied this desire is unfathomable. A meltdown ensues.

And what about the demanding, anger-tinged, profanity-filled rant the hopeful singer unleashes in the hallway after having to exit the audition room minus a golden ticket? The level of self-indulgent expectations revealed by some of these reality-show contestants is downright frightening.

Yet the bad news is that the mentality is sticking. Kids who worship these toxic heroes want to look like them, talk like them, and do what they do. They spend all their time and money trying to find the same purse or buy the exact high-end basketball shoes or get the signature hairstyle. They want to have the same "power" to garner attention from others. At the same time, they too want to be instantly rewarded and have their lives transformed overnight, whether or not they've actually done anything to earn the accolades.

This drastic change in our children's perceptions about life is manifesting itself in their self-stated values. A study published in the *Journal of Personality and Social Psychology* reviewed data gathered from high-school students and college freshmen from 1966 to 2009. The comparison of generations over the years revealed a shift from "intrinsic values" (self-acceptance, affiliation, and community) to a focus on "extrinsic values" (money, image, and fame).

For example, in 1971, when "Baby Boomer" college students were asked to rank how important it was to be very well off financially, they put it as number eight on the list. However, since 1989, being very well off has consistently been ranked number one. As for changing career aspirations, 25 years ago preteens ranked teacher, banker/financier, doctor, scientist, and veterinarian as their top five choices. In 2009, the top five choices had changed to sports star, pop star, movie or television star, astronaut, and lawyer.

Nowadays, corporate recruiters are finding it hard to hire young people at entry-level positions. According to a 2008 report by Ron Alsop in the *Wall Street Journal*, many of those who are recruited "want to be CEO tomorrow." Mr. Alsop cites a survey done by CareerBuilder.com, where human resource executives reported that this generation's expectations included higher pay, flexible work schedules, a promotion within a year, and more vacation or personal time. And once they get their jobs, they continue to need lots of attention and lavish praise, just like Mommy and Daddy gave them. Corporations like Bank of America and Lands' End are going so far as to hire "praise teams" to provide their young employees with the constant affirmation and positive reinforcement they demand.

The End of Empathy

Think back to that last part of the definition I gave you for narcissism: "a lack of empathy for others." A study presented at the Association for Psychological Science reviewed data gathered from almost 14,000 college students over the past 30 years and concluded that the ability of young people to empathize with others has dropped almost 40 percent since 1980.

That's another chilling statistic. I define empathy as simply the ability to identify with another person's feelings. Your level of empathy determines whether you are cruel or kind, sensitive or callous, thoughtful or thoughtless. And what's clear is that so many teenagers today, because they are so consumed with their own lives, just don't have the ability to put themselves in another's shoes and recognize what that other person is enduring. Nor do they even seem to care what happens to that other person. And there's no better example of what's happening than the rise of teenage bullying.

If you think bullying is just one of those trendy, over-exaggerated media stories of the moment, think again. In 2011, the results of the largest study ever conducted on bullying were released. Researchers interviewed 43,000 teenagers between the ages of 15 through 18, and they found that about 43 percent of them said they had been bullied, teased, or taunted in a way that seriously upset them in the past year.

And the bullying and violence aren't limited to fellow students. Do you remember the shocking video that went viral in June 2012 showing a group of 13- and 14-year-old boys who bullied the 68-year-old school bus monitor? The boys attacked Ms. Klein's appearance by calling her "fat," "fat ass," "sweaty," a "troll," "ugly," and "old," and they described her bra size as "triple sag." But apparently those insults weren't cutting enough. They continued, unleashing sexually violent accusations about her raping kids, having herpes, and what might happen if they stabbed her. They punctuated their ugly language with physical harassment, flicking her hearing aid and poking her arm with a yearbook.

As horrible as this scenario was, there are even worse cases. Phoebe Prince was only 15 years old in January 2010 when she hanged herself after being taunted, insulted, and physically harassed by a group of fellow students. The ongoing bullying, done both in person and online, had allegedly stemmed from jealousy over who Phoebe had dated.

Tyler Clementi was just beginning his freshman year at Rutgers University in the fall of 2010 when his roommate surreptitiously videoed Tyler having a private encounter with another young man and then shared it with others. When Tyler learned of his roommate's plan to video him again and stream it live online, he jumped to his death off the George Washington Bridge. These cases are becoming common enough to warrant a new label: "bullycide."

True, plenty of kids do not engage in the actual physical victimization of someone else. But they have embraced an attitude in which they think it's perfectly acceptable to make themselves feel better by verbally victimizing others— taunting and humiliating and ultimately not caring what happens to them.

Is the picture becoming clearer? Do you see what I mean about the overwhelming *sense of entitlement* our children feel, combined with a *lack of empathy* for others sabotaging their lives? The inescapable truth is that we have a lot of young self-absorbed people who have little, if any, sense of purpose. They don't know how to make something of themselves or how to make a difference in the world by contributing to society. And they hang on to this belief that, regardless of their lack of effort, the things they need will eventually be handed to them and life will turn out just fine. Or they figure they can find a shortcut to get them to wherever they want to go.

Is there any way to get them straightened out?

There is, in fact, one answer. And that answer is *you*, the parent. There is still plenty *you* can do to keep your kid from succumbing completely to the travesties of Generation Me. No matter what kind of mess your children have gotten themselves into, *you* can teach them critical, real-world coping skills that will keep them out of future messes. *You* can teach your kids to follow some basic ground rules that will help keep them out of harm's way. And *you* can teach all of your children to think responsibly, make the right decisions, and then create significant lives for themselves.

But to raise such happy and healthy children and to help guide them through all of life's potential pitfalls, *you* have to change, too.

Here are some of the signs to look for that may indicate your child is overly self-absorbed:

- **Expects only the best, regardless of cost.** Designer labels are acceptable; sales or secondhand are not.

- **Needs constant stimulation from external sources.** It is difficult for them to entertain themselves.

- **Craves the acceptance and approval of others.** While they might appear to have lots of friends, many of the relationships are superficial and based on what they can get from each other.

- **Lacks compassion for others' feelings or needs.** The primary focus has always been on their needs and wants, so they have not learned to be sensitive to others.

- **Doesn't appreciate material possessions.** Everything is given to them without effort or work, so it all has minimal value in their eyes.

- **Is self-indulgent without restraint.** No one has ever put limits on their wants and desires, so why should they? Self-control is a skill they neither value nor understand.

If any of this is sounding familiar to you, then you are in the right place. Take comfort! Recognizing the issue is the first critical step in redirecting the course of your children's lives. It is never too late to change. Ideally, you aren't as far down the path as Sarah and her parents. But even they were able to use the arrest and time in jail as a wake-up call. Sarah ended up getting probation and, with the added incentive of jail time hanging over her head, started taking responsibility for her actions. This book will teach you how to do this with your child, too.

2

You're at Risk, Too

I cannot tell you how many times, during my years as a prosecutor, that I met parents who were completely blind to their own role in their children's predicaments. One of my most indelible memories involves the president of an elite West Coast university and his wife who just couldn't see what was happening to their son. I got to know the family when the son was making his first appearance as a criminal defendant in my assigned courtroom. I quickly reviewed the file and then had the detective gather a bit more background. For more than a year, the father had been serving as the president of this prestigious university. The position included the perk of a residence on campus for the president and his family. The president's son—"Tom"—had been running wild on the campus for some time, essentially treating it as his own playground. And apparently, he had been untouchable—until now.

His little world came crashing down when two factors converged. First, the campus police, who had been quietly trying to deal with Tom "in house," had been pushed too far. And second, the son had turned 18: He was now an adult in the eyes of the law. Behaviors that might have been written off as stupid, mischievous pranks on Tom's part now carried a potential prison sentence. Of course, saying this was one thing; actually having Tom's parents understand the new consequences was a whole other bag of problems.

The police report stated that Tom had been seen breaking into a car and taking some property from inside. The value of the stolen property made the crime a felony charge of grand theft, and Tom faced an additional burglary charge for breaking and entering the vehicle. He could get up to three years in prison for this crime. Because this type of behavior was not new for Tom, he and his parents assumed he would get the usual slap on the wrist. But this was their wake-up call.

So, here they came to my office: the university president in his charcoal suit, crisp white shirt, and striped tie (school colors, of course), looking worried and nervous, along with his wife, also dressed in her Sunday best with a strand of pearls around her neck. I inquired as to the purpose for our meeting. The father, in a shaky voice, said they weren't sure what to do for their son and asked if I could give them any insight as to how to help Tom at this point.

It was clear that Tom essentially had spent his youth thinking that he was the one in charge and that his parents were mere pawns to be manipulated. The only reason things were any different this time was that the law had stepped in. Something had to change in order to shake up the status quo, or else Tom would continue escalating his reckless behavior until someone got hurt—either Tom or someone else. And then there would be no turning back.

After Tom's parents took their seats, I took a deep breath, made eye contact with two pairs of red, teary eyes, and firmly told them they were in a critical danger zone with their son. They were on the edge of a precipice, and what they did next would influence the course of their son's future. Now was the moment they had to change their son's life by changing their own lives.

I paused for a few seconds to ensure I had their full attention. "Bottom line," I continued, "is that you need to take Tom out of his environment altogether. He needs to be away from the campus that he has treated as his own little fiefdom, away from his father's name and influence, away from his parents' protective cocoon."

My strong words caused the anxiety level in the room to rise. The father started to explain about the bad group of boys their son had been hanging out with: boys who were up to no good and pulling their son along with them. Without even bothering to argue the point as to who was leading whom down the wrong path, I countered more forcefully, "That, even more so, is why you need to remove him from here altogether. He needs to be in a remote location, away from all the distractions of a privileged existence, stripped down to the basics, where he can learn discipline and rules and consequences."

I could see the suffering that my words were causing them. I softened my tone a bit and told them that I empathized with their plight, knowing how difficult this kind of change was going to be. But I insisted that they really didn't have many options. They were, after all, already at a breaking point. Because of Tom's lack of prior record, he would likely qualify for a probationary sentence with restitution and community service. However, during the years he was on probation, if he broke the law again, he could, and most likely would, be sent to prison on this pending case, in addition to whatever happened on the new case. He would be in a very precarious position that his parents needed to fully understand.

I paused again to measure whether the parents were accepting my counsel. The father finally nodded—slowly, sadly, and with resignation. Then he looked to his wife. She didn't return his glance but rather looked up at me and said in a quiet but unyielding voice, "I can't. I can't let go of him. He is my baby. I just can't lose him."

"You already have. You just don't realize it yet," was my reply.

At that very moment, their son was sitting in the crowded lockup cell behind the courtroom, sleep-deprived in his ill-fitting, county-issued uniform. This was a far cry from the free-wheeling California teen life he had been living. Yet his parents just refused to see what Tom had become. They didn't seem to have any awareness of the negative impact their overprotective coddling was having on their son. They obviously preferred to continue wallowing in excuses, trying to explain away his behavior and theirs, rather than take responsibility and start really parenting him. They didn't see that their desire to keep their son within the confines of their "controlled" environment was actually stifling Tom's ability to learn how to make smart choices for himself and find his own true happiness.

It's sad to say, but Tom's parents were the kind of parents who didn't have a clue.

■ The Roles You Play as Parent

Do you have a clue? Do you know what kind of parent you are?

I know how difficult it is to be a parent, especially these days. There are times when your life with your children seems to be spinning out of control. You are beset by anxiety, bewilderment, and anguish. You can feel incredibly confused, constantly asking yourself just how involved you should be in your kids' lives. Should you let them find their own way, or should you be one of those "Tiger Moms or Dads," always demanding excellence at all costs? I assume you've read about the North Carolina dad who shot up his daughter's laptop to teach her not to post disrespectful comments about her parents on Facebook? Or perhaps you heard about the Family Law judge in Texas who beat his daughter with a belt for using her computer to illegally download music. You probably think, "Heaven forbid! *I* would never be like that."

But then the question persists—"Exactly what kind of parent should I be?"

What many of you have done, perhaps without knowing it, is taken on a "role" that you think will be best for you and your child, all in hopes of protecting your child from potential problems. Some of you have taken on a role in which you tend to give in to whatever your child wants. Some of you have taken on a far more extreme, punitive role. Some of you play the role of the distant parent. Others of you try to be involved in everything your child does.

Let's see whether you recognize yourself in any—or in many—of the following categories.

The Coddling Parent

These are parents determined to protect their children completely from life. They seem to believe it's a bad thing for their children to interact with the world on their own, so they do it all on their behalf. This can ultimately keep kids from developing the capability of dealing with the real world on their own.

Have you been on a playground and seen two little toddlers unintentionally tumble over each other and start to cry? Suddenly, a protective "mother bear" springs from nearby to chastise the offending child who did her baby wrong. Or how about when you attend a school science fair and some of the projects being presented by students look comparable to that of graduate-school caliber? Isn't it always curious that an eager parent always seems to be hovering in the wings, watching over "their" creation with pride? Of course, the one that used to really irk me when I was a single mother raising a son was the Pine Wood Derby races. Some of the cars were breathtaking in their design and speed and clearly beyond the ability of the young child to do alone.

Recently, even an innocuous local community Easter egg hunt became the setting for aggressive meddling by some over-coddling parents. Organizers of the annual Easter egg hunt in Colorado Springs decided to cancel the whole thing in 2012 after parents jumped the rope to make sure that their child got a "fair share" of the loot-filled eggs the previous year. It wasn't like the eggs were hard to find, since there really wasn't any place to "hide" the eggs at the chosen venue. Rather, thousands of eggs were laid out in plain view, inside a roped-off area so that the *young* children could enter with their cute little baskets and fill them up. Ah, such a quaint idea. Instead, as soon as the master of ceremonies proclaimed the beginning of the hunt, parents were literally jumping in, going over the rope to assist their child with the monumentally difficult task of Easter egg hunting.

Coddling parents are also known as "helicopter parents"—always hovering over their child. You see them at nursery school, demanding that their child gets the proper life prepa-ration courses. They carry right on with their coddling as their child hits elementary school and then high school. High-school teachers who use email or texts to communicate with students about assignments and grades are finding that, more than ever, parents are jumping in and using these resources as yet another forum by which to access the teacher immediately about their concern over a test question their child didn't understand or, in their parents' eyes, a grade the child didn't deserve. And the coddling parents are still at it when their young adult goes to college. University administrators are reporting a marked rise in parental involvement in everything from the application process to writing the entrance essays and picking professors, classes, and roommates.

And yes, I'm sad to say, the coddling parent is making its presence known on the job front as well. More than 700 employers who were hiring recent college graduates participated in a survey done by Michigan State University. Approximately 31 percent of the employers reported receiving resumes from parents of the college graduates on their child's behalf, while 26 percent said they were contacted by the parents directly, lobbying for their child to be hired. And get this shocking figure: 4 percent of the employers said that a parent actually *showed up* for their child's job interview!

There is a valuable parenting lesson to be learned from, of all things, baby chicks. When a baby chick is ready to hatch, it will poke a little hole in its protective shell, beginning its long, arduous fight to escape. Sometimes, well-intentioned humans, watching this struggle going on hour after hour, will break the shell and pull the tiny chick out. Sadly, most of those chicks end up dying. Why? Because that struggle was a crucial part of the chick's physical development. It prepared the chick to survive on its own.

Not long ago, a Yale-educated New York mother of two boys named Lenore Skenazy decided to let her 9-year-old son ride the subway alone. When she wrote about her experience in a newspaper column, she found herself the target of harsh public judgment about her fitness as a mother. Many found it irrelevant that Lenore said she was a safety fanatic regarding helmets and seat belts. They found her completely irresponsible, letting her son try the subway on his own, despite that she provided him with a map, a metro card, and money for an emergency.

I admit, I would have been very hesitant to let my son ride the subway alone at the age of nine, but then he didn't grow up in New York where riding the subway is a regular part of a child's life experiences. And if he had expressed a burning desire to ride the subway alone, as Skenazy's son did, I would have carefully considered the risk and made my own assessment, balancing possible dangers with the opportunity for him to grow up and build his own confidence. I certainly would not have immediately said "no!"

As Skenazy so aptly described it in her newspaper column, we are coddling our children into "hothouse, mama-tied, danger-hallucinating joy extinguishers.... Ten is the new two. We're infantilizing our kids into incompetence."

Yes, the world is a more dangerous place, and yes, as parents you want to coddle your children more than ever before to keep them safe. But to all you well-meaning coddlers, I pose this question: Is this the way to build self-esteem, inner confidence, and the ability to function in any number of life circumstances? How can your children start to flourish when you are holding on to them so tightly?

A young nursery-school teacher was watching some of the boys who were trying to jump out of a tree. When she started to tell the boys to stop, the head mistress of the nursery, an older woman with years of experience behind her, gently shushed the new teacher, saying firmly, "One day these boys will be jumping out of planes. We have no right to instill fear in them at this age."

I have a friend who has spent her life coddling her now young adult–aged daughter, who had some learning disabilities early on in childhood. In response to her constant fretting, I have told her more than once, "She will be successful, in her own way and at her own speed, *if* you will step back and *let her.*" My friend's "aha" moment finally came last year, when she was once again spending massive amounts of time and energy meddling in her daughter's life, even though her daughter had not asked for help. She was mid-sentence justifying her actions because of her concern over the daughter's capabilities to function on her own. I stopped her and said, "Didn't I just see pictures on Facebook of your daughter bungee jumping off an extremely high bridge, grinning from ear to ear, with the caption 'Best day of my life!'? Is this the girl who you still see as not being able to manage for herself?"

My friend stopped and thought for a minute. A rueful smile came over her face, as she shook her head slowly. "Yeah, I see what you mean." They *will* succeed, if we will *let* them.

The Permissive/"Cool" Parent

A close relative to the Coddling Parent is the Permissive/"Cool" Parent—the parents who do not want to say "no." They justify their behavior by saying "I want to give my child everything *I* didn't have growing up. I don't want them to feel deprived the way I did. I want their childhood to be enriched."

Permissive/"Cool" Parents are usually loving and responsive to their children. It is extremely important to them that their children love—and like—them back. And they believe that the easiest way to get that love is by refusing to set boundaries. Obviously, these parents have given very little thought to the question "When does too much of a good thing become a bad thing?"

We have all seen Permissive/"Cool" Parents in action: the mothers who let their children run like banshees through the restaurant without any consideration for those around them; the fathers who push the grocery cart down the aisle throwing in every item their child asks for, whether it is healthy or not;

the parent who buys the designer dress their daughter insists on for prom, regardless of the hefty price tag.

As ironic as it might seem for a Permissive/"Cool" Parent, boundaries are critical in childhood development. Initially, it is actually pretty simple. Your baby just wants to eat, sleep, and be dry and warm. So, give your baby what she *wants*, because that is also want she *needs*. But, starting with toddler age, your children are now going to start developing *wants* that aren't necessarily what they *need*. "I want that toy!" "I want to eat ice cream all day!" "I want to touch the fire!"

This is when parents must move to the next developmental stage and begin to set boundaries. Rules should be established and explained. Over and over again, you find yourself saying "no" and "We don't do that because...." Is it exhausting? Yes! Frustrating for parent and child? Of course. But it must be done for the child to make healthy progress. Children begin to understand that the world doesn't revolve around their "wants."

So, why do some parents miss or avoid this significant step? There are several reasons. They don't like confrontation. They don't want to be rule-oriented. They don't want to hamper their children's free spirit. They want their children to see them as a friend and confidant. They want their children to like them. They want their children and their friends to think of their house as the "fun" house. They believe that their children will be more open and communicative with them if they are "cool." They remember how completely uncool their own parents were, and they have decided to be different.

Unfortunately, permissive and overindulgent parenting usually ends up stunting the maturity of the children in ways that the parents never intended. If children aren't given limits by their parents, it is hard for them to know how to set limits for themselves. Unintentionally, the permissive parent is sabotaging the development of their child's self-control and goal-setting skills.

In the end, the child doesn't feel any better about who they are. One of the most ironic outcomes of Permissive/"Cool" Parenting is the child's difficulty in being able to be happy.

What amazed me during my years as a prosecutor was just how many of these young defendants had been pampered by their parents. Very few of them appeared to be "bad seeds" from the get-go. I will never forget a young man I met from an upper-class, luxurious world who, according to all that I was told, had been a talented, outgoing boy. But as the years passed, his grades failed, his ambition withered away, and his once-engaging personality turned rude and sarcastic. He began to act as if he was owed such favors as special privileges, late curfews, and extravagant allowances, and when his parents didn't oblige him quickly enough, he got angry. Soon, he became defiant, and it was only a matter of time before his rebellion against authority led to breaking the law.

Why did this young man, who was raised with everything he wanted, still get in trouble? Like so many other children of over-indulgent parents, he never learned to appreciate what he had been given. He grew up feeling entitled. Because his Permissive/"Cool" Parents refused to set limits, he developed an inflated sense of his own power and freedom. He felt shielded from the consequences of his reckless actions. He expected to be accommodated, and he was not going to let anyone—or any law—get in his way.

Learning how to deal with disappointment and frustration is an important skill for every teenager to acquire. Not knowing how to handle sadness or distress may result in your child eventually taking extreme, destructive measures to avoid anything that might be negative or difficult. Lying, cheating, or running away may become that child's coping mechanisms for life's challenges.

Add it all up, and that kid is destined for a very precarious future.

The Competitive Parent

Competitive Parents can be found pretty much at any forum where kids are competing with each other: golf tournaments, Little League games, pee-wee football, swim meets, piano recitals, spelling bees, beauty pageants, and on and on. For some parents, the race to have "children who win" often starts even before that little bundle of joy is born. How many of you read one of those ever-so-helpful "what to expect" books while you or your partner were pregnant? These books have become very popular for their insight and their information, but as well for their outlined "stages of development" so we can begin to gauge our child's progress in relation to what the book tells us that every other embryo of the same gestational period is doing.

In fact, as soon as our children make their first foray into this big bright world, it is like the starting gun is fired and we are off! Height, weight, length, "Apgar tests"—parents start comparing these medical measurements as a way to size up how their baby matches up to other babies, and they haven't even left the hospital! Then, with every follow-up doctor's appointment, more "scores" for their child's "performance" come in as they learn what percentile their baby is in for head circumference and growth development.

Granted, these measurements are not, on their own, harmful. Grades, assessment tools, evaluations, competitions, races...none of these things is inherently evil. They are meant to help parents. And the truth is that encouraging and supporting our children to succeed and achieve is an important part of the parental role. But why do some parents use them to crow about their child's superiority or, conversely, to fixate on ways to push their child to get ahead of all the other children? And what effect does this fixation have on children as they get older and reach the cusp of maturity?

Plenty of parents get involved in their child's life not just to help the child progress and grow but to feed some internal need of their own that isn't being met. In an almost unconscious way, they want to compensate for their own insecurities or past failures. Some overly competitive parents try to live vicariously through their child either because they feel their own childhood was lacking or, conversely, because they want to extend their own charmed childhood. In a misguided and dysfunctional way, they believe they are doing the right thing by pushing their child to the limit.

As a result, we see parents shelling out thousands of dollars so their 2-year-old can go to "camp" to be immersed in Mandarin Chinese or French. Second-graders (future Hemmingways, to be sure) can hone their writing skills at the John Hopkins summer program. Granted, these programs are amazing—as long as the children are there because they *want* to be, not because their parents have put them there to give them an edge on the competition at a very young age.

And then there are tutors. Hiring a tutor to help your child pass a difficult class in high school or to prepare for college entrance exams has been a common practice for years. But now it's regular practice for parents to get tutors for their children in middle school and even elementary school.

If that's not enough, let's not forget the overabundance of *after-school* activities that competitive parents make their children participate in. Sports, music lessons, language classes, dance practice...the list goes on and on.

Whatever the parent's motivations, the impact on the child can be extremely damaging. Beginning in elementary school, counselors are seeing manifestations of *burnout* in children. They are exhausted, agitated, and unable to focus. They have difficulty settling down, getting along with others, and managing their feelings.

The long-term effects are apparent as the over-scheduled child tries to navigate through college. The years of high expectations and constant multitasking result in young adults who are rushing around, who are feeling out of control and out of balance, and who are always worrying that they are falling short. There are reports that the need for mental health services on college campuses has increased so dramatically that student health offices and counseling centers have been unable to keep up with the demand.

Many times in my court cases, I saw what happened when young people were pushed to the edge by a competitive parent's never-ending expectations. I'll never forget one case that played out like a Greek tragedy. "Sam" and "Mike" were college seniors from good families—successful families who had high expectations for their sons' futures.

Sam and Mike planned on going to law school after college. They both knew that where they went to law school depended on how well they scored on the LSAT, the national law school admissions test. Most prelaw students spend months studying for the exam. But for some reason—maybe they didn't want to do the work, they didn't have confidence in their own abilities, they just wanted that edge over everyone else, or they didn't want to let their parents down—Sam and Mike decided that they were going to do something different. They decided to cheat their way to a near-perfect LSAT score.

The complex plan required purchasing a fake ID, recruiting some accomplices, buying some pagers, and flying to Hawaii to take the LSAT. After all the work, it looked like Sam and Mike had actually pulled it off—their test scores placed them both in the 99th percentile. However, a combination of their suspicious behavior during the exam and one of their accomplices getting caught and confessing led to their arrest and prosecution for conspiring to commit a felony.

These two young men, with so much promise and so much expected of them, cracked under the pressure. It was just too much. How sad to think of all that they might have accomplished if they had exerted that same amount of planning and innovation to a worthy endeavor—something legal. And how sad that someone along the way didn't make sure they took a step back to find some balance in their lives.

Ultimately, competitive parents forget to teach their child to enjoy living in the present—to interact with others in a non-structured setting. It is one thing to want to expose your child to a well-rounded range of opportunities. It is another thing to pile on the activities to the exclusion of rest and play. Remember that? Playtime? Research shows that "play" is crucial for our brains to be creative, to achieve more nuanced connections, and to, literally, be more thoughtful.

Dr. Stuart Brown, a psychiatrist and founder of the National Institute for Play, has concluded from his studies that "play" is fundamental to enhance such things as learning, memory, and well-being in our children.

Indeed, play does a world of good for a kid. If you're a competitive parent, it would be nice if you scheduled in a little noncompetitive playtime as well.

The Punishing Parent

Perhaps you're a parent who has clearly defined rules for your children about what they can and cannot do. That's great. But—and here is the key question that you are on the honor system to answer truthfully—do your rules and standards result in you interacting with your child in a negative, judging, critical way? Is your focus more on where they failed than how they succeeded?

If it is, it could very well have to do with the way you were raised. Older generations of parents believed that giving children lots of praise was a waste of time and ultimately would make them soft. They lived by the philosophy that children were to be seen and not heard and that they were to obey without question or hesitation. And if they didn't, it was entirely proper for them to get a tongue lashing—or worse.

In a sad way, it is always interesting to watch children who have been living for a long time under the reign of a parent who, even for the best reasons, pummels them with negative comments and messages. The constant parental disapproval tears down their confidence. They begin to feel unworthy, unaccepted, and never good enough, and they lose that glimmer of hope that they might someday make their parents proud of them.

You can tell the children who live under Punishing Parents just by the way they carry themselves, trying to not take up too much space. You can hear it in the way they mumble, worried that what they say is going to be criticized. You can tell they don't feel important enough to look you in the eye.

And this is the case even for kids whose Punishing Parents regularly toss out statements like "Hey, I love you" or "You understand it's because I love you and want the best for you that I get on you, right?" You may think that a positive comment balances out a negative one. Well, guess what? The actual ratio is five to one: It takes five positive comments to make up for one negative comment. According to Dr. John Gottman's well-known research on marriages, communication patterns in happy, healthy relationships have five times as many positive interactions as negative ones. We all hear, feel, and remember the negatives much more strongly than the positives.

When my friend's daughter was about 3 years old, she was quite a handful. In desperation, my friend found herself starting to use the good old "If you don't finish all of your eggs, Santa Claus won't come on Christmas Eve" technique in early November. At first, it worked great. Clearly, her daughter was at the perfect age where the whole Santa thing filled her with excitement and awe. The first few times my friend reminded her that Santa's performance was conditional on her behavior, she immediately did what was being asked of her. But by the time Thanksgiving had gone by, her little daughter had probably heard the Santa threat two or three times a day. One day while they were out shopping, her daughter was lagging behind, getting distracted by this and that like most 3-year-olds do. My friend uttered those words one more time: "If you don't stay up with me, Santa isn't going to come." Much to her surprise and chagrin, my friend's cute little girl plopped herself down right in the middle of the busy aisle, and as big tears welled up, she said to her mother, "I don't care anymore if Santa comes."

Unwittingly, my friend had broken down her sweet rambunctious daughter with one too many negatives. As great as her daughter's desire was to have Santa come down her chimney, she just couldn't take the potential punishment hanging over her head anymore. In her own young mind, she was trying the best she could, but it just wasn't enough.

Think for a moment about how you speak to your child. Yes, you are the adult, and you're in charge. But do you wield your authority with respect? Do you grant your children the dignity that every human being deserves? Or do you find yourself criticizing them and their personality in big broad strokes instead of focusing on a specific mistake?

Do you get so irritated with your children's failures that you hold them in contempt, speaking to them sarcastically, mocking them, or teasing in a mean-spirited way? Do you ever fly off the handle or lose control?

One day I found myself sweltering under an unrelenting sun, watching my teenage son, an accomplished golfer, compete in a critical tournament. Each player had to complete the course twice, and as any golf aficionado will tell you, playing 36 holes on a tough course all in one extremely hot day is no walk in the park.

After his first round, my son and I grabbed a sandwich and sat down at a picnic bench, along with several other competitors. Suddenly, the still air was disrupted by a harsh, male voice. We then heard two sharp smacks. Stunned, we tried to process the scene that was taking place about 20 yards from where we all sat. One of the young female players was standing, her head down, arms by her sides and fists clenched, while an older male figure, standing just inches from her, bellowed his disapproval of her performance. To punctuate his total disgust, he had slapped her twice, full force with his open hand, right across her face. As he pulled his arm back to strike the young girl again, some of us began yelling for him to stop, while others ran toward the man and grabbed him. The young lady just stood there in silent compliance until someone pulled her away.

My son just gently shook his head and said quietly, "That's her dad." That stopped me. "Her dad?" I asked. "Are you kidding me?"

"Mom," he replied quietly, in that teenage inflection that stretches that one short syllable over three notes—high, drop low, then ends in the middle range. "It happens all the time. My friend Paul had a bad round in the last tournament, and his dad made him go straight to the driving range and hit balls for hours in the rain right after to make up for his bad score. Some parents are just like that."

Yes, children are resilient. They will try over and over again to make their parents proud of them. But when their parents continually withhold love and approval, the children don't wonder what's wrong with their parents. Instead, they think that they, the children, are to blame.

But eventually, as the children of a Punishing Parent get older, their survival mechanisms for the continued criticism will change. Their attitude becomes one of pessimism, negativity, and cynicism. Some turn their anger inward and become depressed. They retreat from the world out of fear of being rejected yet again. Others take that pent-up frustration from never feeling good enough and act out in self-destructive ways, finally fulfilling their parents' negative views of them. They search for substitute forms of love and approval, finding euphoria and a false sense of invincibility in a drug- or alcohol-induced high or engaging in reckless sexual relationships.

Or, in an attempt to assert their independence, they begin to look for other ways to protest—and that's when so many good kids begin to commit petty crimes. Instead of the parental coercion making the children obey, it makes them rebel, which then leads to more coercion followed by more rebellion: a never-ending cycle.

So, those of you who, with the best intentions, lean toward being a Punishing Parent, please remember this: No one blossoms under criticism or contempt. The bottom line is that teens who feel rejected are on their way to deeper and deeper problems.

The Deaf Parent

It is a common parental complaint that our kids don't listen. How many times have you said to your child, "Stop what you're doing and listen to what I'm saying"? Now think for a moment, how many times has your child said the same thing to you?

No parent deliberately tries to play the role of the Deaf Parent. Still, it happens all the time. The reason many children don't listen to their own parents is because the parents do not actively engage in listening to their own children. "Hold on," you may be saying. "What does listening to my kid have to do with getting my kid to listen to me? I am the parent, and he is my child. My child *has* to obey me; I don't obey him."

I agree; it is the parent's role to make the rules. That is the pecking order of the household, so to speak. But—and this is an important *but*—communication is a different animal. For it to be effective, it must be a two-way street. It involves as much listening as it does talking. And the truth is that few parents know how to really listen.

Think about it. We are constantly bombarded by parenting experts on all sides advising us to *talk* to our children. *Tell your children about the dangers of drugs, teach your kids the importance of hard work, sit down with your kids for the dreaded sex talk.* But if you haven't already been *listening* to your children, long before these discussions ever pop up, they certainly aren't going to suddenly sit down and willingly listen to *you*. The all-talk parenting style does not foster a genuine interest by children in what you are saying, nor does it teach children how to express themselves when called upon to do so. The end result is almost always teenagers who couldn't care less about what their parents are saying. They become remarkably adept at tuning their parents out, and they have no inclination or ability to convey their own thoughts or feelings to their parents.

When it comes to communicating with our children, almost all of us parents start out with the best intentions. We spend hours when they are just infants trying to read their faces and their body language, endeavoring to understand what message they are trying to convey.

Then come those first unforgettable words out of our children's mouths. When they master "Mama" and "Dada," we beam with delight and pride.

Before we know it, however, those little rascals have mastered that one dreaded word: "Why?" And soon, we are developing selective hearing skills. We tune out the constant chatter. That frequent whiny tone becomes like fingernails on a blackboard. We are busy. We are tired. And let's be honest, we don't *know* all the answers to the never-ending stream of curious questions. So, unless we want to take the time to Google every inquiry, we start hedging our responses—or we answer their questions in an irritated tone of voice. "Conversations" become repetitive commands or judgments from the parents and not much more.

Subtly, we are sending our children a message to stop bothering us. "We don't really want to hear what you have to say," we're essentially telling them.

We have all seen parents pushing their child's stroller down the street, chatting away on the cell phone glued to their ear. Or we've seen parents sitting on the park bench, busily sending emails on their iPhones while they brush their kids away with a curt "Go play." Granted, it's nice to have the parent there physically with the child. But, without the element of communication, the connection is so limited. Indeed, being a Deaf Parent is one of the simplest ways to disconnect from your child.

"Listening" is a skill that I find a lot of people lack, even in my own profession. You would think that lawyers, who are trained to be expert communicators, would recognize the value of listening and develop this critical expertise. *Au contraire.* It is a pet peeve of mine to watch a brilliant trial attorney question a witness in court, dazzling the audience with eloquent phrasing, a large vocabulary, and dramatic intonation. The attorney finishes the question and waits for the witness to respond. An answer is given. It is intriguing, puzzling, a bit unexpected, and, if one listens closely to the witness's hesitancy, perhaps incomplete. The witness pauses tentatively. My mind explodes with follow-up questions—probing queries that veer from the meticulously prepared written script sitting on the podium before the questioning attorney. Questions that will subtly probe that almost imperceptible opening the witness left, pushing the witness to expand and explain. But instead, the "brilliant" attorney, who is wrapped up in the artistry of his own questions, plods on to the next question listed, letting the opportunity slip away.

How many of us do the same thing as parents? And honestly, how many of us had parents who essentially did the same thing? Most of our parenting models consisted of adults laying down the law, dictating the rules, and that was the end of the discussion. While that style might be easier for the parents, studies show that for kids to actually *accept* and *assimilate* their parents' counsel, they need to feel like there is a pattern of listening and communicating already established. Ever wished you could grant your child greater self-esteem and confidence? You can. Just listen to them.

The Stressed Parent

Here is another role that no parent tries to emulate. But it's one of the most pervasive. It's the parent who is consumed with stress.

I remember taking a written "stress test" in one of my college psychology courses. The directions indicated that if five or more of the factors had occurred within the last 12 months of my life, I was at risk for a nervous breakdown.

I was more than a little shocked when I realized I had checked off way more than five boxes. I really hadn't taken the time to think about all the stress in my life.

The Holmes and Rahe Stress Scale is a bit more detailed than the test I took in college. It includes several additional indicators to consider, and each one has a point value assigned to it. Why don't you take the test? The following are various factors that bring stress into your life, with their designated point value. Which of these factors has occurred in your life over the past 12 months? Circle the ones that apply, and then add up your score.

Death of your spouse	100
Divorce	73
Marital separation	65
Jail term	63
Personal injury	53
Marriage	50
Fired from work	47
Marital reconciliation	45
Retirement	45
Changes in family member's health	44
Pregnancy	40
Sex difficulties	39
Addition to family	39
Business readjustment	39
Change in financial status	38
Death of a close friend	37
Change to a different line of work	36
Change in number of marital arguments	35
Mortgage or loan over $10,000	31
Foreclosure of mortgage or loan	30

Change in work responsibilities	29
Son or daughter leaving home	29
Trouble with in-laws	29
Outstanding personal achievement	28
Spouse begins or stops work	26
Starting or finishing your degree	26
Change in living conditions	25
Revision of personal habits	24
Trouble with boss	23
Change in work hours, conditions	20
Change in residence	20
Change in schools	20
Change in recreational habits	19
Change in church activities	19
Change in social activities	18
Mortgage or loan under $10,000	17
Change in sleeping habits	16
Change in number of family gatherings	15
Change in eating habits	15
Vacation	13
Christmas season	12
Minor violation of the law	11

According to the test's creators, if you score 300 points or more, your stress level puts you at "high" or "very high" risk of becoming ill in the near future, 150 to 299 points puts you at "moderate" risk for illness in the near future, and 150 points or less indicates you're a "low to moderate" risk of illness due to stress.

So, what was your score? More than 300 points? Less? And just think if the test included some additional factors (as I think it should) that reflect some common stressful events we experience in our modern world—for example, a terrorist attack, a natural disaster (tsunami, fire, earthquake, flood, etc.), or being the victim of a violent crime. Just imagine how many points you'd rack up.

Stress, obviously, permeates our modern lifestyles. We get up in the morning after having slept a few fitful hours, far less than the six to eight hours health experts tell us we need. We breathe in air filled with toxins, and we eat food sprayed with poisons or made out of chemicals. We endure stressful commutes to get to our stressful jobs. Thanks to all the social media, our expectations for what our lives should look like are grander than ever, pushing our standards for "happiness" higher and higher.

I could go on and on about all the stress we face in our lives. But here is what's critical for you to remember: The stress that you deal with every day has a significant impact on your children.

Sure, you say, you know that stress has some effect on your life with your kids. Some days, because the pressure at work has gotten to you, you come home and explode at your kid for not doing his homework. You release your frustration on your child, even though deep down you know they aren't the real problem. But once you've calmed down, you figure it's all behind you, right?

Wrong. Not to stress you out more, but the level of stress in your life can deeply affect your children in a way that will last their entire lives. I'm talking about potentially drastic physical, mental, and emotional consequences. Your stress is no longer just your issue. It is your child's issue as well.

You know how experts will tell pregnant women to sing or talk to their fetus? We see fathers rubbing mommies' pregnant bellies and interacting in a calm, loving way with their unborn child. That is because, even in the womb, our children are sensitive to us—our moods, our emotions, and our tones of voice.

Okay, you say, it makes sense that a fetus is going to feel the stress and emotions of its mother while it is inside her womb. But once the baby is born, isn't that literal physical connection broken? A baby isn't developed or sophisticated enough to detect tension and stress around them, right?

Actually, babies are amazingly sensitive to the moods of their parents. Babies have to rely on their parents for their survival. They respond to the warmth from cuddling and swaddling, and likewise they can become fussy or inconsolable when there is strain and agitation around them.

Indeed, after reviewing numerous studies, Dr. Andrew Garner confirmed that babies and children are "very sensitive social barometers" and that "when parents stress, the kids are going to be stressed." Dr. Sandra Weiss found in her own research that children as young as 2 years old were more likely to exhibit psychological distress when their mothers showed signs of psychological distress.

Surprised? If you have been underestimating the impact of your stress on your children, you aren't alone. The results of a 2010 Stress in America Survey released by the American Psychological Association revealed the drastic impact of parental stress on children. Ninety-one percent of the 1,136 children surveyed, ages 8 to 17, were aware of their parents' stress when they did such things as yell, argue, or act too busy to even recognize their children were around them. And the reported impact of parental stress on their children was disheartening: 39 percent of the children said they felt sad, 39 percent worried, 31 percent frustrated, 24 percent annoyed, 21 percent helpless, 13 percent were angry, and 13 percent felt alone. Only 14 percent said it didn't bother them.

Talk about disconnecting from your kid—without intending to! It is time to stop thinking that stress is just "our issue" to deal with. At the very least, stress makes parents less capable of giving calm, positive attention to their child. Living with stressed-out parents, the kids are left to come up with their own solutions about how to cope. Many of the tweens and teens report that they seek out sedentary comforts, like listening to music, playing video games, or watching TV.

More troubling is the statistic that drinking, the use of marijuana, and the abuse of cold and cough syrup to get high is on the rise in teenage girls. The primary reason given by the girls themselves? Wanting to reduce stress at home.

And just to put the nail in the coffin, so to speak, let me tell you what "toxic stress"—adverse stress that continues over a long period of time—can do to your child's *brain and hormones.*

Perhaps you have seen or heard the commercials that talk about the evil hormone cortisol that is to blame for your belly fat. Well, in actuality, cortisol is just one of the hormones that is released by your body in response to stress. Consistent exposure to cortisol and other stress hormones can impact the brain of your developing child in several ways:

- The stress hormones can damage the brain circuit connections and even result in a smaller brain.

- Elevated stress hormone levels, including cortisol, can weaken the person's immune system, which can cause chronic health problems.

- Continuously elevated cortisol levels can cause damage to the hippocampus, which is responsible for learning and memory, and the damage may last into adulthood.

And just recently, the results of a multiyear study revealed that parental stress actually altered the DNA of their children. Scientists at the University of Wisconsin, Madison, measured the stress levels of parents when their children were infants and again when the children were between 3 and 4 years old. Then, when the kids were 15, they analyzed their DNA. They found that high stress in the mother during their child's infancy altered 139 genes. Dad's high stress during the child's preschool years (when typically the dad would become more involved with the child) altered 31 genes.

The genes that were affected, usually by being "silenced," included a gene that signals insulin, a DNA-repair protein, and two protein genes that aid in brain development and behavior.

So, let's recap. Stress, which we parents think we are dealing with on our own, is impacting our children in huge ways. It distances us from our kids and their needs. It triggers negative emotions in them. It leads to them modeling our unhealthy coping mechanisms. Moreover, it is causing physiological damage to their brain and DNA development that may stay with them their entire lives.

And ultimately, when we are stressed, we have little time to actually focus on our children and see what is happening in their lives.

■ Embracing Real Parenting

None of the parenting roles you play are completely *wrong*, of course. But the best parenting involves taking on a much grander role—one that lets you effectively pass on the best life skills to your children, teaching them how to stay away from self-destructive behavior as well as inspiring them to aspire to find true happiness in personal achievement.

And that's where we're headed next.

Your Parental Checklist

Do you, like the university president and his wife, have a difficult time facing reality concerning your son or daughter? Do you have trouble recognizing what is happening in regard to their behavior? Do you have trouble recognizing your own behavior?

Here are five questions to ask yourself that will begin to help you get on your own road to reality with your kids:

1. Do you feel inadequate to confront whatever problem your kids are facing? Do you feel uncomfortable discussing certain subjects—like sex—with your children?

2. Are you desperate to avoid the so-called social stigma that you think might occur if word leaks out that you have a problem with one of your children? Do you tell yourself that your son or daughter is not as troubled as the Smiths' children down the street?

3. Are you hesitant to give your kids "absolutes," telling them that certain behaviors are right and certain behaviors are wrong because you don't want to be "uncool" and out of touch? Do you avoid bringing up the subject of values with your children? Do you find yourself putting more emphasis on your kids' outward image—like their popularity or ability to do well in sports—rather than focusing on building inner character?

4. Do you feel completely confused about how to discipline your children when they do bad things because they are now teenagers and just one step away from adulthood? Do you think such actions will cause your teenagers to turn away from you?

5. Are you afraid of getting honest with yourself about your own problems—like your own drinking or drug use or lack of anger management—which in turn keeps you from pushing your children to get honest with themselves? Are you afraid for your kids to see the real "you" because you think they will no longer love you the way they did when they were young children?

Parenting Notes

Parenting Notes

Part 2

The Principles:
Building a New Life from the Inside

3

Starting at the Core

Let me tell you about my parents. I'll be the first to admit that I was lucky when it came to parents. My father was a sociology professor at UCLA and a licensed marriage and family therapist. He did a 30-year longitudinal study on what makes a marriage work, and he wrote lots of books on addictions and drug abuse. My mother decided, right in the middle of raising seven children, to go back to school and get her master's in counseling psychology. I have many memories of being Mom's homework guinea pig, with her administering intelligence tests and personality tests to me.

My parents adopted all seven of us kids from a variety of racial and cultural backgrounds. Their character and values shaped their parenting style. My parents emphasized compassion, thoughtful communication, sensitivity to others' feelings, and education for the purpose of being able to help others and contribute something positive to the world. Concepts like integrity, honor, and character were a regular part of the family discussions. We didn't chat about a person's outward appearance or their wealthy or worldly accomplishments, but rather we focused on people's life experiences and how that might have shaped their personalities or approach to life.

As a result, I fell very comfortably into my psychology major. After all, those people spoke the language I had grown up with. One class in my psychology curriculum particularly resonated with me—the behavior modification course. In it, we were assigned to train a live chicken to perform specific tasks, following the Pavlov theory of consistently rewarding the desired behavior and ignoring or immediately punishing the negative behavior. Pavlov was brilliant! The training worked like a charm. I decided then and there that I would train all my future children in a like manner and, obviously, with the same successful results.

I moved fast. By the time I was 18 years old, I was a year and a half away from a bachelor's degree in psychology, and I was engaged to a guy from my hometown—someone smart, athletic, and hardworking who reminded me of Robert Redford. On my wedding day, I remember thinking, wow, my whole life is before me, and everything is coming up roses!

But a year and a half later, at the ripe old age of 19, I was a college graduate with a degree that I couldn't readily translate into a job. I was also separated from my husband, and I had just become a new mother to the most amazing little baby boy. Literally, the graduation, birth, and separation had occurred within the space of three weeks.

I felt like the world had stopped spinning on its axis. The "me" I knew was gone, and instead—practically overnight—I had become a confused, scared *mother* who felt like she couldn't even breathe, much less function. I was drowning in the depths of postpartum blues, compounded with good old run-of-the-mill depression. In a very short time, my carefully thought-out and focused life plan had been sucked down the garbage disposal, and I was left hanging. What was I going to do? Where was I going to go? How in the world could I be a good parent in this situation?

I was so overwhelmed that I would hold my son in my arms and wish that I could put him back in my tummy where he would be safe until I could figure out this mess my life had become.

Obviously, life didn't turn out to be any easier for me simply because I had good parents. I made plenty of mistakes and got myself into some complicated predicaments. But because of the environment my parents had created at our home—and because of the lessons they taught me—I knew that I would get back on my feet. And I did. I went to law school, found a law career that I was passionate about, and at the same time made sure my son came first.

Believe me, I'm not sitting on my high horse here. When I was raising my son, I too made some big mistakes. In fact, after 48 years of living, I know that my biggest regrets all fall under the heading of spending way too much time at work and not enough time just being with my son.

But I also know that I passed on to him—just as my parents passed on to me—the vital qualities that enabled him to deal responsibly and confidently with the inevitable struggles of life. I made sure he felt loved and important, and I made sure he had a strong mental-moral core.

The Power of the Mental-Moral Core (MMC)

So, we start at the core. You may be wondering, "The core of what?" Well, let me explain with a scenario that will ring a bell. When fitness experts talk about getting healthy and in shape, they inevitably say, "It all starts with your core."

I remember when I first heard that mantra. My core? What is my core? Do you mean sit-ups? I hate sit-ups! And so I ignored my core for a few more years. But I kept hearing the message. It was getting louder and more persistent. Finally, I decided to listen a little more carefully. I found out that the core actually includes your torso, which is your mid and lower back, your abdomen, your neck, your pelvis, and your bum. These are the muscles that essentially link your upper body and lower body together. Thus, no matter what movement you want to make, whether it is to shoot a basket or ride a wave, that movement is going to go through your core. As a result, if your core muscles are weak or inflexible, the performance of your arms and legs will be impaired.

So, what does this have to do with our children? It is a crucial component that I observed to be missing in most of the parents that I worked with in court—a focus on building their children's core. Not their physical core, but what I call their "mental-moral core." It is the center of your child: the mental muscles that every life event that your child faces will pass through, but only *if* it is developed.

Why do I call it "mental" and "moral" core? The "moral" aspect refers to the ethical code by which we live. For some reason, nowadays just saying the word *morals* seems to evoke sighs and eye rolling. It's ironic that so much of society shuns the idea of talking about morals because—guess what?—we all have a moral code, whether we admit it or not. Everyone has this cluster of ideas, feelings, and experiences inside of them that, taken together, is that individual's belief system of what is good and bad, what will make them happy or sad, and how they should act accordingly.

"Mental" is important to include because it gives a specific location for our morals. Often, when people do speak about morals, they sound like lofty ideals: goals to put up on a shelf to gaze at admiringly. Not here. When I say "mental," I am emphasizing even more strongly that this moral center is not only the core of your child, but it is ingrained, embedded in their thinking. It becomes their state of mind.

If the MMC is developed in your children, then they will have a focus that will shape every step of their lives. It gives them a game plan so they can act with confidence and decisiveness. It gives them the wisdom to make good choices and to be productive adults with a passion for life and the world around them. On top of that, their MMC gives them the strength to stay balanced and keep moving in the right direction when they hit uneven terrain. It lessens the risk of them falling down.

You know that old cliché: It is what's on the inside that counts. Well, cliché or not, it's true. And that is where our parenting should start as well.

There are four cornerstones to strengthening one's MMC:

- Be honest.

- Do it yourself or do without.

- Choose your own values and then become them.

- Be motivated by your inner desires, not by fear or a desire to conform to others' perceptions.

Be Honest

In my experience, *honesty* stands first and foremost as the guiding principle of life. It defines the shape of every act you make. It is far-reaching in its scope and influence. And it does not include exceptions. It does not allow you to say to yourself, "I will be honest...except for padding my resume. I will be honest...except when I'm paying those unfair taxes. I will be honest...except when I call in sick."

It is those exceptions that put you on the path to losing touch with the truth. Many times our inclination is to avoid momentary awkwardness with little fibs. While it may not be our intention, these little fibs easily progress into thinking it is easier to say whatever will get us our instant gratification, regardless of what is true. But down the road, this disregard for the truth becomes a desensitization to the truth and ultimately an inability to see or even remember what is true. Look at Bernie Madoff, Scott Petersen, or John Edwards. So many bad choices begin with dishonesty.

Of course, no one is or can be perfectly honest at all times in all dealings. There are times we might soften our true opinion when asked if we like a new haircut or if someone's thighs look big in a given pair of pants. But the key is to instill in our children the *mentality* of approaching life honestly. Making the commitment to be honest in all areas of life gives your child a bright standard. It takes fortitude and determination, but it produces confidence and mental clarity.

Do It Yourself or Do Without

There is nothing more empowering for our children than to have engrained in their core the mentality of being capable of doing whatever needs to be done themselves.

When a child grows up with this attitude of self-sufficiency—when they approach each problem with the attitude "How can I accomplish this?" rather than "Who is going to do this for me?" they are not sitting around expecting others to coddle them, provide for them, or figure life out for them. They are proactive. They have an inner pride and sense of control that comes from being able to make things happen.

But there's a second part of self-sufficiency, which is just as important as the first—and that is *doing without*. Your children may not be able to obtain something they want no matter how hard they work for it. Or it may take years to get what they want. Thus, for so many children, when an object of desire is not immediately available, they get stuck, fixated on the unattainable. But if your children are able to cope with not having something they want, then they're freed.

Doing without is a concept that many parents never even consider teaching their children. The focus is always on getting, getting, getting, without realizing that learning to do without fosters increased appreciation for what the children already have. It also allows for them to develop creative adaptive skills to figure out how to manage without the item or find an alternative solution. For example, if, rather than automatically receiving the latest cool car on their 16th birthday, a teenager has to do without until saving up the money to purchase a car themselves (or go "halvies" with their parents), that child will become very industrious in figuring out ways to get to football games and parties. They will learn the value of hard work and independence. And when they finally earn that car, they will cherish every penny's worth.

Choose Your Own Values and Then Become Them

Building your children's MMC means guiding them to find values that they will incorporate into their personal identity. When helping your children to choose their personal values, it might be helpful to use this exercise: Have your kids look at some obituaries, and notice how every person's life, after all the years, comes down to a few words—how their family and friends describe them. Then ask your children to think far ahead into the future, beyond their careers and their own kids. After all is said and done, how would they want their friends and family to think of them? What three words would they want to be used to describe them? Benevolent? Kind? Ambitious? Humorous? Generous? Successful? Loving?

Have them choose three words. And then start talking to them—daily if you have to—about how they are putting those three words into practice and making them a reality. Ideally, with the long-term perspective in mind, your child will choose commendable characteristics. But if they end up with words like "rich," "famous," and "beautiful," hold back on the judgment and probe further. Have them describe for you what that means, what it looks like, and how they would get there. With some thoughtful discussion, perhaps together you can find some deeper values that they can connect with.

Be Motivated by Your Inner Desires, Not by Fear or a Desire to Conform

So many of us are motivated by fear, such as fear of punishment or fear of failing. Some of us eventually become motivated by others' approval or receiving acclaim in society. Still others of us are motivated by a desire to follow the rules, whether they're religious dictates, cultural mores, or government-imposed laws.

At some level, all of these forms of motivation can work to produce the same result—good, healthy behavior. However, there is another source for motivation that elevates their lives to a higher and far more rewarding plane. It's a motivation that comes from their own free will:

> *I am choosing this course of action not because the law tells me to or because my parents are watching me or because I don't want to get grounded—I am choosing to act this way because it is what I want to do, what I know will make me happy. I will act "good" because I am "good." I will give to this charity anonymously because I feel good when I help my community, not because it will make others think I'm generous. I will take care of my sibling because I love her, not because my parents told me to. I will not cheat on this exam because I would know that the grade wasn't truly mine.*

Teaching our children the importance of making decisions based on their true character gives them a reservoir of strength to guide their decisions, no matter what challenge or trial is thrown their way. Rather than filtering their choices through extraneous factors such as how others might judge their actions, they will look inward and determine what decision will be most consistent and true to their own character.

Inspire Your Child to Aspire

These four cornerstones of the MMC will give your children a solid foundation that will ground them throughout their lives. Is it heavy stuff? Absolutely. As a parent, you will need to simplify the concepts according to your child's age and level of understanding. It may take years for them to fully grasp what you are trying to teach them. They may rebel at times. But you must always work on building those muscles. Just like a successful personal trainer, you must show your child how to use the correct form. And then help them practice, over and over again.

And as any trainer will tell you, a critical component of success is getting a client to believe that they can, should, and will succeed. A trainer must inspire his client to aspire. And that's exactly what you have to do too.

I love the word *inspire*. To me, it's far different from the words *encourage* or *motivate*, which focus more on what the encourager or motivator is doing or saying to push another person to act. When you inspire someone else, you are helping him to find the power within himself to achieve. The Google definition refers to "fill(ing) someone with the urge or ability to do or feel something."

And to "aspire" is to do more than just hope or dream. To aspire means to eagerly seek out, to desire something of high value.

In short, I want you to *inspire* your children to *aspire* to find their passion in life, to rise up and to thrive in the world. I want you to inspire them to aspire for true, inner joy—not the fleeting thrill that comes from getting a new outfit or being the star quarterback or the momentary pleasure derived from public accolades. But rather, inspire them to aspire for true accomplishment from their own hard work. Help your children get to a place where they are spurred to live out their dreams without fear of failing—or fear of ridicule.

This may sound overwhelming, but don't get discouraged. It is a process that is ongoing throughout your child's life. It involves shaping your child's mind-set to look beyond where they are now and move confidently toward where they want to be. One great way to teach your child this concept at any age is to help them find good heroes.

Who are your child's heroes? Do you know?

From the time they are toddlers, our kids are continually trying to figure out who they want to be when they grow up. A big part of that journey is finding and emulating individuals who appear to have all the things that they want to have. Heroes are a great way to teach your child what they can do with their lives and how they can contribute to society—in other words, how to find their own meaningful life path.

Do some searching yourself. Find people, famous or not so famous, who are doing good things. Talk about them at dinnertime. Praise them. Express excitement and interest in their accomplishments. Stretch your child's concept of who qualifies as a hero and what qualifies as a heroic act.

People magazine does a regular article called "Heroes Among Us" that highlights ordinary people doing extraordinary things—but extraordinary, in these stories, often means small things that have a huge impact. Sharing these types of stories with your kids can plant a seed of all the good they can accomplish themselves without having to become famous.

So, parents, inspire your children by exposing them to true heroes. And encourage them to follow their own path with passion.

4

From Self-entitlement to Self-control

Remember how, at the beginning of this book, we talked about one of the major issues affecting Generation Me is that kids want what they want and they want it now? It always brings to my mind the spoiled child from the classic movie *Willy Wonka & the Chocolate Factory*, Veruca Salt. Every time that spoiled little rich girl came on the screen, she was demanding that her accommodating father get her one more thing: the first golden ticket, a golden goose, an Everlasting Gobstopper. And what parent can't hear her whiny request for her *own* Oompa Loompa ringing in their head?

We see the modern-day version of Veruca everywhere: spoiled high-school seniors driving expensive cars that their parents bought for them, tweens carrying absurdly high-end purses, even kids who come to school late and without their homework done because they persuaded their parents that they were "stressed" and needed to sleep in.

So, here comes the big question: How do you teach your kids self-discipline and self-control? Rather than fostering an attitude of self-entitlement, how do you cultivate your child's ability to regulate oneself, to be able to work within set boundaries, and to live with self-control?

It starts with setting limits, saying "no," and then following through on the consequences. It means letting your child fall down. Essentially, it involves all the things that the well-intentioned, over-indulging parents of the last 30 or so years have purposefully not done. It is hard for many parents to see their child get hurt, feel bad, or deal with negative consequences. However, when a child faces the consequences of their own actions, whether they are positive or negative, that child begins to understand the benefits of exercising self-control. They will be able to see that developing the discipline to make the wise, prudent choice now will pay off in the long run. But when a parent constantly intervenes, the child misses out on the growth they would make from experiencing it themselves.

Self-control grows when you give your child responsibility over their life and allow them to make their own choices. It is a key component to your child's future quality of life.

■ The Marshmallow Test

If you want to understand how vital self-control is for your child's "how to survive and succeed in life" kit, then let me tell you about the marshmallow test.

In the late 1960s, a clinical psychologist at Stanford University named Walter Mischel came up with a simple scenario to test a child's level of self-control. The study involved 4-year-olds. A proctor offered each child a beautiful, white, fluffy, delectable marshmallow. The proctor then told the child they could eat the marshmallow right away, *or* if they waited until the proctor returned, they could have *two* marshmallows to eat.

The proctor left the room. Some children immediately ate the marshmallow. Others distracted themselves with other things until the proctor came back. Still others struggled to hold out, fixated on the marshmallow, staring at it, playing with it. Few were successful at not eating their marshmallow. Only about 30 percent of the 600 kids tested were able to wait the full 15 minutes until the proctor returned with the second marshmallow.

In 1981, Mischel followed up with those same children, who were now in high school. He wanted to see what had happened to the children who had eaten the marshmallow quickly and what had happened to the children who had waited. The new data revealed that the less time the child had been able to wait before eating that first marshmallow, the more likely they were to have behavioral problems at home and at school. They had difficulty with paying attention and maintaining relationships, and they especially had trouble coping under stress. Children who had been unsuccessful in waiting for the second marshmallow were now less decisive, less confident, and more stubborn than the children who waited.

And here is the staggering statistic: The kids who had been able to wait the full 15 minutes for the second marshmallow in the original test, averaged, several years later, a full 210 points higher on their SAT scores than the children from the original test who lasted only a short time before biting into their marshmallow.

It's not just frustration that results from a lack of self-control. Without realizing it, parents who don't teach self-control are setting their children up for failure in their adulthood. Here are just a few of the issues that children who exhibit a lack of self-control end up struggling with as adults:

- Physical health issues (poor lung function, sexually transmitted infections, obesity, high blood pressure, bad cholesterol, dental disease)

- Substance dependence (tobacco, alcohol, marijuana, other illicit drugs)

- Financial difficulties (savings habits, home ownership, investments, retirement plans)

- Credit and money management issues (bankruptcy, missed payments, credit card problems)

- Breaking the law

Serious, life-changing stuff, right? In the long run, kids without self-control tend to fall apart, their lives characterized by irresponsibility and excessive freedom. But kids with self-control—kids who have been taught how to handle frustration and other so-called hot emotions—tend to stay on track and eventually flourish.

Self-control is a valuable and crucial asset for all children, even the most privileged kids in America. I read an interview of a famous acting couple where they discussed their parenting philosophies. They explained that while they acknowledge to their children that Mommy and Daddy are rich, they make a point to tell the kids that *they* are not rich. The expectation for them to work and earn their own way is discussed and incorporated at a very basic level. They even tell their kids that their bedrooms aren't "their" rooms but are "borrowed" from their parents, so they are expected to take good care of them.

All parents need to instill an expectation of self-control in their children. You *can* give them the opportunity to develop into outwardly focused, appreciative, productive adults.

But first things first: You have to let go of focusing on controlling their lives and focus on them developing their own self-control.

The Power of Delayed Gratification

When I was growing up and I asked for something that my Dad was saying "no" to, he would always finish up his refusal in an irritatingly cheery tone with "Just think—this will strengthen your frustration capacity."

Sadly, very few of today's parents have any inkling that their children *need* to strengthen their frustration capacity. They aren't even trying to teach their children self-control. Instead, they are more focused on how much work it is to say "no" to their child. They don't want to deal with all the conflicts when their children are angry at being deprived. Or they don't want to disappoint their child or deny them something that "everyone else has!" In the end, it's a lot easier for these parents to hope that their kids get the message about delayed gratification down the line—preferably when the kids are older and out of the house.

As we see from the marshmallow test, the foundation to self-control is learning how to delay self-gratification. And how do you teach this to your children?

Ideally, you start when your kids are young. When Jessica or John wants something, instead of just automatically handing it over, use clear, concise directives to explain to them how and when they will get it.

- "I will give you the toy *when* you finish making your bed."

- "I will come play with you *when* I'm done doing the dishes."

It is pretty easy as long as you stick to your guns the first few times. As small kids, they understand exactly what the deal is. And when you, the parent, follow through like you say you will, not before the condition you required and not later than what you stated you required, then your children can catch on fairly quickly. There might be an initial power struggle by your child to see whether they can force you to follow their timetable instead of yours—in other words, a temper tantrum, crying, incessant demands—but if you hold firm, everything will pay off. Once they see that their whining has no effect, they will learn to do what will actually get them what they ultimately want.

What you've done is begin to build another of your child's MMC cornerstones: *Do it yourself or do without.* Your children are learning how to earn something, rather than, literally, just having it handed to them. What's more, building this cornerstone when your children are young becomes nearly priceless when the children turn into teenagers.

But what if your children are already teenagers? Is it too late, considering they are being bombarded with promises of easy fame and fortune from every angle: television, movies, social media, and their iPads? Absolutely not. The same process applies, but be patient because their attention just may not be as focused.

Stay firm and consistent. One of the best ways to do that is to give them plenty of "when" directives. "I will let you drive to school *when* you come up with your share of the insurance money." "I will let you go have lunch with your best friend *when* you finish cleaning your room as you promised."

If they continue to whine or nag about immediately getting the things they want, you must stay calm, not get emotional or distracted, and *refuse to budge.* In a completely dispassionate manner, do not give up and give in—otherwise, the next time there is a power struggle, your child will keep pushing even harder. And it is amazing, no matter whether your child is a toddler or a teen, how long they are able to keep pushing to have it their way. So, hang in there and keep your eye on the long-term pay-off.

And what if your children lose interest in their initial request? That is a good thing! They are learning to distract themselves with other things so they can delay their desire without being overcome with frustration. Make sure you still follow through on your directive so your children learn that their patience will be rewarded and that they can trust what you say.

■ The Power of Accomplishment

I tend to favor biographies when I choose a book to read because I am always fascinated by seeing how people choose to live their lives and then observing what results from those decisions. When I read biographies, I am also struck by a particular theme that I find to be common in the lives of people who have achieved great success. They all write about how they had to learn to deal with mistakes, failures, and rejections over and over again, before finally getting their big reward. They emphasize how they learned to pick themselves up and keep moving each time, which ultimately set them on the road to true achievement.

Did you know that Steven Spielberg was denied admission to the University of Southern California film school? So, he went to Cal State University in Long Beach instead and eventually became one of the stellar directors of our day. J.K. Rowling, author of the *Harry Potter* books, had her first manuscript rejected several times before Bloomsbury Publishing finally took a chance on it. Early on in Elvis Presley's career, he was fired by the manager of the Grand Ole Opry after just one performance, with the parting shot "You ain't goin' nowhere, son." At the age of 65, Colonel Sanders decided to market his fried chicken recipe. He drove around the country for two years, trying to find someone who was interested. He was rejected 1,009 times. Can you imagine the fortitude it took to keep going?

That, right there, is what so many of our children miss out on—true achievement, which comes from trials and challenges and struggles and, yes, losing. All of the cajoling and hand-holding and adoration that we do as parents will never instill the strength of character that comes from experiencing struggle. Such events are invaluable learning opportunities for our children to prepare for the future when they'll have to deal with thornier, more complicated situations completely on their own.

One day I came home from work and heard my teenage son cold calling potential customers. He had taken a summer job of selling high-end knives. I listened quietly from the other room, not wanting to interrupt. Three times in a row, I heard his side of the short conversations, all ending in rejections. I'll be honest—I wanted to run into that room, grab the phone away, and throw my arms around my son in a protective embrace. How could those faceless people so callously reject my son's efforts? But I restrained myself, and my son continued, plowing through more "no's" and hang-ups.

A few years later, he moved on to door-to-door sales, one of the most rejection-filled occupations I can think of. Soon he was experiencing a high level of success. More than the money, the accomplishment confirmed in him the mind-set that he can achieve whatever he dedicates his efforts to, even if it includes some rejection along the way.

If you're still struggling with the concept of letting your kids fail, I understand. We all want our children to experience overflowing joy and abundance. But you're being naïve if you think you can impose things from the outside that will create internal satisfaction for them. What you need to do is help your children seek their happiness from *within* themselves— finding a sense of self-esteem from their own actions and their own accomplishments and their own service to others. These are things they actually can control and choose themselves. They can find stability and peace in their own lives with the knowledge that they have been able to pull themselves up from their bootstraps and do things for themselves. Expecting others (which usually means their parents) to provide every-thing, including their happiness, will only lead to a lifetime of discontent.

Goal Setting

It's important to get your children to talk openly and without embarrassment about goals they would like to accomplish— such as getting to school on time, going to a concert, or even getting accepted into Harvard. Here are some suggestions:

- Help them break their goal down into the steps that will get them there. If they want to buy a car, for instance, have them answer these questions: How much money will I need to save each month to be able to buy the car by a certain date? What costs will I need to cover once I buy the car? Make it a col-laborative process by helping your child figure out solutions they can manage for how to get things done. They should feel responsible and in control of the process from the beginning.

- Help them to commit to the goal by memorializing the com-mitment. Writing things down is an extremely effective tool to help your children stick to a goal or a promise. The act of writing forces them to think through their goal in detail and then keeps them focused on what they have committed to doing.

- Make sure they have written deadlines to accomplish that goal. Studies show that kids who set deadlines for themselves actually perform better than those who don't.

- Once the goal is set, your role should be aimed at positive reinforcement. No child is too old for positive reinforcement. Instead of jumping in when they are struggling and doing some of the work for them, set up small positive reinforcements to keep them going. Such reinforcements will be constant reminders that the work they are doing is worth it.

5

The Golden Rule of Respect

Many parents struggle with parenting because they don't think their children respect them enough to listen and learn from them. Here is something to consider—most kids *don't* respect someone they think can be manipulated into giving them everything they want, especially their parents. Instead of being role models that they look up to and want to emulate, parents become targets for their children's irritations, frustrations, and then exploitations.

Teaching your children about respect is a crucial key to overcoming the flaws of Generation Me.

There are two parts to teaching your kids about respect:

- Treating your child with respect

- Being worthy of their respect

Treating Your Children with Respect

Model what respect looks like and how it feels for your child by treating them that way. It is the easiest and clearest way for your child to understand what you want them to do. Easier said than done, right? We all readily agree that children should show respect to their parents. But often adults overlook the importance of extending that same courtesy to their children.

When I was 10 years old, I was assigned to watch my 4-year-old sister while my dad worked in his home office. At one point, my little sister got rambunctious and started screaming in a playful way. My dad, irritated at the interruption (and prone to acting first and asking questions later), burst into the room and immediately ordered me into a timeout in the bathroom. I obeyed, indignant yet silent. About ten minutes later, Dad opened the door. By then, my sister had confessed that she had just been playing, and I had done nothing wrong. At that moment, my dad, being the adult, could have just brushed the whole thing off and told me to come out. Or he could have gone a bit further and cleared me of any blame. Instead, he did something that changed our whole relationship. He apologized for his mistake, and then he pulled out his wallet and asked me how much the time I had spent in the timeout was worth. I was stunned and speechless. He pulled out a few dollars and handed them to me and then went back to work. I cannot tell you how important and significant my dad made me feel at that moment. Treating me as someone of value and worthy of his respect, even at the age of 10, made a lifelong impression on me.

It isn't always easy to treat your children with respect, especially when they start making choices and acting in ways that are very different from you. What should you do when you see your kids diving headfirst into the latest eyebrow-raising teen fad, whether it's lip piercings or pink hair? What should you do when they play music that you find positively disgusting? What should you do when they use language—whether it's in their texting or in their real-life conversations—that you find highly inappropriate?

Every generation, of course, wants to be inventive in expressing its differences from the previous generation. Just like we did eons ago, our children talk about how we, their parents, don't understand them or their lives. They think of us as dinosaurs when it comes to such issues as underage drinking and sex. They think we're ridiculous to be offended over their Facebook lingo.

The first step to connecting with your child is to take a trip down memory lane and recall our own childhood when we, too, were trying on various personalities until we successfully formed our identity. Why? Because that's all your children are doing. They are on their own "identity journey." Your children are going to take some risks in finding out who they really are. And no matter what you do, you're not going be able to stop them. You can make sure your kids are wearing the "proper" clothes or hairstyles when they leave the house. You can make sure they don't listen to music with violent or highly sexualized lyrics in your house. You can refuse to let them watch movies that show illicit, immoral behavior. You can tell them not to use certain profane words in front of you. But that's not going to stop their journeys to find their identities.

Here is one of the hardest parts about parenting: You may rightly feel, because of your own life experiences, that you have better insight into your child's strengths and weaknesses and therefore know which life path is best for them. But the greatest gift you can give your children is the respect and freedom to create their own lives.

Of course, it's only natural that we have preferences for what our children do with their lives. A family of doctors might dream of their child growing up to become a doctor. Parents who have built their home around a certain religious belief might prefer that their children follow the same religious tenets. Republicans might prefer that their children also choose to be Republicans. It is normal for parents to want their children to follow in their footsteps.

But it is imperative that you create an environment where your children can find themselves and discover their own path, all the while knowing you are right there, loving and supporting them along the way. You are showing respect for their ability to find their own identity.

With all their knowledge about life, relationships, and families, my parents respectfully allowed me to discover my own identity, even when it was difficult for them. When I was in high school, I decided that I wanted to try out for the cheerleading team. This desire caused my conservative parents—and yes, they were very conservative—quite a bit of consternation. They didn't see a lot of value in it, and my mother disapproved of the short skirts. I think in the back of their minds (battling with their own preconceived notions and stereotypes) they thought it would be a gateway into the world of "shallow" popular kids.

But for me, it was much simpler. I loved to dance, and our cheerleaders did lots of dance moves. After many closed-door discussions, during which I crouched with my ear against the wall trying hard to hear, my parents agreed to let me try out. They did throw in one caveat, which perhaps, deep down, they didn't think I could overcome. I would have to pay for everything myself. With the costs for uniforms, shoes, summer camp, and matching camp outfits, the total price tag was going to be hundreds of dollars.

Little did they know what they had created. I had been playing the piano since I was five. So, to raise the money I needed, I began teaching piano lessons at $10 an hour. During my free time, I practiced my tryout routine for hours out on the back patio, where I could see myself in the glass doors. The whole family groaned every time I rewound my cassette tape (yes, I'm that old) and started the music again.

The auditions were held in the school gym, so the entire student body could watch. When the day of the tryouts finally arrived, I walked in so nervous I could barely process all the people and the noise. I glanced around the crowd, and there, way up in the corner at the very top of the bleachers, were my parents. I was shocked. And embarrassed. This was, after all, high school, and they were the *only* parents I could see. I had no idea they were going to be there. They weren't the kind of parents who typically had time to come to all of my games or concerts. But then I realized what they were doing. They were making a point that they were going to respect and support my dreams. And long story short, I made the team.

Evolving as Your Child Evolves

Essentially, parents must embark upon the long process of giving up their control of their child's life and replacing it with a respect for their self-control. One parenting expert described the different phases of parenting like this—you begin as the Benevolent Dictator, transition to a Compassionate Counselor, and finally become Research Assistant.

You start out as the Benevolent Dictator to your young children, being their sole source of their sustenance and nurturing. You decide when they will eat, when they will sleep, and what activities will fill their time. They're totally dependent upon you.

However, as they grow more aware, you begin slowly relinquishing control. You let them start to make their own choices. You allow them to face the consequences of those decisions. You are slowly turning the reins of their life over to them. Showing them that you have the respect and confidence in them to manage their lives with self-control will reinforce their desire to do it responsibly.

Then, as your children establish their place in the world, you evolve again. Now, with them having their own careers and families, you must become a dependable, trustworthy Research Assistant, providing objective information for your children but always remaining at arm's length, lovingly and respectfully.

■ Be Worthy of Your Child's Respect

I want to make sure you caught that. The best parenting role does not *only* mean you stop coddling your kids or you stop punishing them inappropriately or making them the target of your own stress. It doesn't *only* mean that you will take the time to teach your teens the right kind of discipline and values. It means that you *yourself* will lead a healthy, disciplined, value-driven life that your kids will see and want to model with their own behavior.

And believe me, they're watching you. Despite that it feels like they're living in an alternate universe, one that you're not allowed to enter, you do remain the constant in their lives. Sure, at the moment, they might seem enthralled with rejecting parental authority. They might, at the moment, proclaim loudly that conforming to your lifestyle means a surrender of their identity. But the unvarnished truth is that *you* still remain more significant than anyone else in their lives—and that includes their best friends or the latest fashion or the hottest new band that's making the scene.

What's more, whether you like it or not, you remain the most powerful role model in their lives. Indeed, they are always checking out what you do and say. They are watching how you handle your own stress and provocation. They are seeing how you set goals for yourself and what you do to accomplish them. And they are noticing what character and devotion means to you. Their brains are copying behaviors that they see from you over and over.

As a result, if you make adjustments in your behavior, your kids inevitably will too. If you change, they'll change.

■ Parents Can't Be Hypocrites

If there's one thing I've learned in observing and interacting with kids of all ages and their parents, it's that the children who have respect for their parents are the ones who have a much higher chance of rising above the turmoil in their lives. They have higher odds of becoming solid young adults, imbued with self-reliance, self-control, and solid morals.

Now, let me be blunt. Even when your kid respects you and the way you conduct your own life, you're hardly home free in the parenting game. Parenting a child today is often a conflict-based relationship even under the best of conditions. Even the finest kids on the planet will do things that will make parents want to pull their hair out.

And on the flip side, let me add that no parent will ever be perfect—none of us will even get close. No matter how honorably you lead your life, you're going to screw up in front of your kid at some point. You're going to say something inappropriate, something that's going to hurt, or something that's going to cause your child to withdraw or, in their own way, rebel. And then, no matter how hard you try, you'll probably end up doing it again.

Nevertheless, what I've learned is that in a parent-child relationship based on respect, things always come back around. If your kids respect you, they will inevitably turn to you for help, guidance, reassurance, and, yes, inspiration. They will see you as their personal lighthouse, a constant beacon of reliability and love for them to turn to when they are struggling with the terrible storms of adolescence.

Creating that kind of relationship—that magical mixture of nurturing and firmness—is not easy. There is no "respect formula" that I can lay out for you. Nor is it a quick journey to reach that kind of respect. You're going to need persistence, focus, and commitment. And you're going to have to behave with your children in ways that perhaps you've never behaved before.

The data is really undeniable. *The American Journal of Public Health* released a stunning report claiming that one out of every four children in our nation sees family alcoholism and alcohol abuse while growing up. Yet most parents hardly see the irony. What they focus on are the headlines like the 2009 study that revealed 10.4 million young people between the ages of 12 and 20 reported drinking alcohol in the last month, or the 2011 study that reported 33 percent of teens have tried alcohol by the eighth grade with a jump to 70 percent by the twelfth grade, or the finding that binge drinking is prevalent among our children, with 15 percent of eighth graders, 36 percent of tenth graders, and 51 percent of twelfth graders in the study reporting having been drunk at least once.

Clearly, we have a huge problem when in just one year, there were almost 190,000 underage teens reportedly injured in alcohol-related accidents that required trips to an emergency room. These are horrendous numbers. But what kind of blinders do we have on if we refuse to admit that it's the parents who are showing their own children how to behave? It's the ultimate "do as I say, not as I do" parenting style—and that's a style that never works.

Some of you right now may be shaking your heads, thinking that this whole chapter is totally unrealistic. You might think it's fine for there to be one standard for the adults and one for the children, and here I am, advocating that parents actually change their behavior to conform to what the children should be doing. You might be saying, "Hey, parents are adults, and they should get to act like adults—just as long their children don't know."

Sorry to burst your bubble, but your children have an uncanny ability to sense what's going on in your lives. If you try to keep a separate life that isn't consistent with how you are raising your child, you are risking your foundation of honesty, trust, and respect with your child. When they find out that you're living your life in a way that conflicts with what you've been advocating, then the children begin to question and doubt all the principles on which they have built their mental-moral core. If they sniff just the slightest scent of hypocrisy, your authority begins to crumble. They want to either copy your behavior, rebel because of it, or use it as an excuse to discount every single word you say.

Take a moment and answer the following questions:

- Are you being honest in all areas of your life—at home, with your children, in your work?

- Are you living free from any kind of addiction, including alcohol, drugs, sex, and work?

- Are you managing your stress, anger, and frustration in healthy ways?

- Are you making good decisions, working from your mental-moral core?

- **Are you conscientiously working on your own moral values?**

- **Are you committed to speaking about people behind their backs the same way you'd speak to them face to face?**

- **Do you live the same moral standards you expect your child to uphold?**

- **Do you honor commitments and promises you have made to your spouse and your children?**

If you didn't answer "yes" to all of these questions, then you need to change. And let me assure you, I'm just as imperfect as you are. My own most painful parenting mistakes came from thinking that "talking the talk" with my son was enough. I am very emphatic about this point because of the number of parents I met who didn't seem to recognize how their own hypocritical behavior had damaged their child's life. One day, when I was a prosecutor, I received a call from a mother, "Anne," about her teenage daughter, "Hannah." Anne explained to me that her once sweet, loving daughter had started sneaking around with a group of kids that Anne didn't know, engaging in high-risk behaviors like shoplifting, minor vandalism, and excessive drinking. Anne said she had worked hard to raise her daughter the proper way, talking to her about what was right and wrong, and discussing the importance of good values. Alarmed by Hannah's wild behavior, Anne sat down with her and firmly explained to her that stealing, destroying property, and underage drinking were crimes for which she could be arrested. But instead of deterring her behavior, Hannah continued to escalate her recklessness, trying to avoid detection with layer upon layer of lies.

Anne said she had tried to punish Hannah in various ways, but that only made Hannah more devious and sly about her activities. Anne even attempted to give her rewards and bribes for positive behavior but still couldn't distract Hannah from the thrill she seemed to get from breaking the rules. Anne finished by saying that she would do anything to help her, but she just didn't know what to do.

As we talked, it became clear that Anne, herself, had a drinking problem and that she was also being sneaky about her own private behavior. Hannah, I realized, was simply following her mother's example.

Of course, the best behaved parents can still have children who struggle and go wayward. We all know there are no guarantees in this parenting business. But if you're letting your own personal behavior slide sideways, then you are significantly raising the risk that your children's behavior will go sideways too.

You must always ask yourself the difficult questions. Is there something you are *doing* that, despite everything you say, is signaling to your children that it is okay to act the way they're acting? When you ding the car parked next to you, do you brush it off saying "It was just an accident" rather than leave a note? When the clerk gives you too much change back, do you keep it, saying, "It was his fault, and I don't want to drive all the way back"? Do you leave the tags on clothes so that you can return them after you wear them? When something comes up that you don't want to do, do you come up with a lie to get out of it, maybe even asking your child to convey the lie for you?

As parents, you can't afford to bury your head in the sand about the impact your personal choices may have on your kids. You have to go "all in" with the parenting game. This isn't a part-time job. You must walk the walk seven days a week, twenty-four hours a day. You have to be reliable and consistent with your children—and, above all, you have to be honorable, or else everything falls apart. It may be hard to do, but what is even harder is realizing that your "own personal decisions" have brought upon your child turmoil and uncertainty. Until you experience it, you can't imagine the agony that comes from seeing your child in great pain that you have caused by your own selfish choices.

So, get your life in order. Whatever it takes, do it. Your kids are worth it.

6

Listening to Your Children

Given the dynamics of the parent-child relationship, a simple conversation can sometimes become a very exhausting exercise. First, there is usually a gap of at least 20 years or more—which means there may be parts of the parents' language that are not understood by the child, and vice versa. Second, the parents tend to be overly focused on maintaining their position of authority, while the children's willingness and ability to communicate are greatly impacted by their age and raging hormonal changes.

It sounds like a stalemate, right? Not at all. When parents tell me about how difficult it is to "talk" to their child, then I tell them the answer is to "listen." The problem with the lack of communication between parent and children is not the lack of talking—it's the lack of listening.

The truth is, there needs to be a lot more listening going on in our homes, not just by those of you who have fallen into the role of Deaf Parents and ignore just about everything, but even by those of you who think you are doing a good job listening.

■ Redeveloping Your Listening Skills

When I was in the middle of a jury trial and needed to listen intently to a witness, I had to shut out everything else going on in the courtroom: the jurors writing in their notebooks, the defendant whispering to his attorney, the judge shuffling papers. I would subtly encourage witnesses to talk by making sure they felt comfortable with the pace and the tone of my questions. This was the only way witnesses would really open up enough to share what they knew.

Do you see the parallels? As busy parents, we don't often put that high of a priority on listening. That takes time and energy we just don't have. We are goal-oriented, so communication is for the purpose of us telling our kids what the plan is and then making sure it gets done. So, what's the big pay-off for listening? I'll tell you. Listening is what gets your child to talk.

Okay, I know if you have younger children, you are saying in protest, "Loni, the last thing I need right now is for my child to talk more!" You are probably bombarded with an endless stream of chitter-chatter interspersed with repetitive questions. I feel your pain.

For any of you who still have younger, rambunctious children in the house, let me take you aside for a moment and encourage you to take three deep calming breaths. Then let me grab you by your tired shoulders, shake you awake enough to look me in the eye, and warn you that *they will be gone before you know it*. Now is the time to give it all you've got. That means you must make that extra effort to listen to the story about the class snake that escaped and the cloud in the sky that looked like a princess. You must try to answer why the grass is green and why you can't see the wind. Follow along when they are complaining about Brittany S. and Brittany T. and Brittany W.

Why? Because then, when the big stuff comes along—the sex questions, the breakups, the friends who are starting to use drugs—your child will be one of the lucky ones who knows that they have someone they can trust who won't be too busy or too tired to listen. So, no matter how mundane or seemingly inconsequential their talk is, listen to it. You will likely learn things about your children. On top of that, you will build greater intimacy with them while they still want to let you in. And, in turn, you'll teach your children the valuable lesson that when they speak, you, the parent, will listen. Their words have value to you.

If you stay in touch with your children by listening to them, it will pay off big-time during the critical teen years. And if you aren't there yet, don't get down on yourself. There's still time to re-connect those valuable lines of communication. In some ways, your kids are still like they were as toddlers, tugging on your sleeve, desperate to be heard, ready to tell you their tales about the joys and sorrows in their lives, their fears and aspirations. But first you need to step away from your own frenetic lives and self-absorbed thoughts. You need to shut out all the other noises and listen to whatever your children say. Go so far as to tell them that you want to be a better listener. And then show them with your actions by...listening.

Modeling the Listening Skill for Your Children

By listening, you are (here is that word again) *modeling* for your kids the skill of listening. They will see how it is done. They will understand the various steps to good listening. Most of all, they will know how good it feels to have someone who wants to listen.

Just remember, you don't have to be perfect at listening, because there is no such thing as a perfect listener. Each relationship is different, tailor-made to the personalities involved. My mother, for instance, raised seven children, kept the house clean, made dinner every night and homemade bread every Saturday, sewed our dresses...you get the picture. You'd think she wouldn't have had time to listen to much of anything. Yet some of my earliest memories are of me and Mom hanging out while my older brother and sister were in school. Mom would iron, and I would talk and talk and talk. She was multitasking, but I still felt that she was listening. Later, as more kids came, she would always tell us we could talk to her, but we had to follow her. That usually meant talking while sitting on the edge of the bathtub while she scrubbed the toilet or talking while setting the table as Mom made dinner. She was a master at being able to follow a conversation no matter what the circumstances.

My father, on the other hand, had a very different style of listening to his children. He worked a lot, and when he was home, it was not his style to just sit around and shoot the breeze. However, he would schedule weekly meetings to talk with each of us kids. It was not necessarily the classic warm, fuzzy scenario, but we knew that we had access to Dad and that he would schedule us in.

Another key point to remember is that you must be a flexible listener.

When your child gets older, listening becomes more of a strategic balancing act. A few kids at this age, usually girls, will eagerly babble on to their parents about everything. But most teenagers will start exerting their independence by shutting down verbally. Sometimes, as a parent, it feels like you are walking over a minefield, trying to gingerly feel when to push further and ask more questions and when to hold back. My suggestion is that you try to show an interest in what your teenager is doing, while being respectful of their need for space. My sister, who taught high school for many years, calls this skill "casual awareness." You are fully aware of what matters to your teens, but you ask just enough questions to be pleasant and give them a shot at talking about it, without intruding.

On the other hand, beware of the "fake interest" approach. Teens detect it easily, and they resent it. If they feel that you are just giving them lip service, they will shut down. So, invest some time in learning a bit more about whatever it is that your child is interested in, outside of just asking questions like "Oh, really?" Do some homework—look up videos or articles or watch their favorite show to gather some background so you can come back to the table with something interesting to add to the discussion. It will show your teenagers that you really do care about them, and that will go a long way with them.

One more suggestion: Be mindful that, just like you, your children have times when they are talkative and times when they are not. Don't be disturbed if your child is not a morning person and wants nothing to do with conversation before school. Nor should you push it if you get little to no response to your long list of questions that you tend to ask when your kids get home from school. ("How was your day? What happened in algebra? Did you turn in your assignment in English? What's going on with your friends?") For some of you, their silence is going to make you think they are hiding something. Not true. They may simply be out of their "talking rhythm." They just need to retreat, decompress—to chill. By evening, they might be open to a casual conversation on how their day went. On the other hand, some kids come home from school bursting with excitement or frustration and wanting to vent. Try to be sensitive to your own child's talking rhythms and, if possible, make the effort to be casually available during those times.

Another great listening time is in the car, driving your kids around from one thing to another. Rather than talking your kid's ear off because you have a captive audience, think about leaving space for your child to just ramble. And remember, if you are also driving your kid's friends, you can really learn a lot by keeping quiet and listening to what they say.

■ The Beauty of an Intriguing Question

Here's one more technique that helps both parents and children practice good, focused listening: formal questions at dinner. Some parents ask their kids to come to the dinner table with a current event to discuss. What a great way to kill a bunch of birds with one stone—encouraging an awareness of the world around you, practicing intellectual thought, getting insight into what your child finds to be interesting, and providing opportunities to share insights and values in real-world scenarios.

Other families go around the table, with everyone taking turns at dinner sharing their "highs" and "lows" of the day. This not only stimulates discussion but allows parents to do some empathetic, supportive listening.

The key here is to be consistent in having dinner together and maintaining the habit of discussion. My mother loves doing "the questions." She finds intriguing, thought-provoking questions, types them up on slips of paper, and puts one under each plate at the dinner table. Everyone has to take their turn and answer the question under their plate. Some people will give a quick, one-sentence response. Others will share things you never knew about them even though you have lived with them for years. And it gives everyone in the family a moment when they have the floor where everyone else has to listen.

Six Tips for Effective Listening

Let me preface these tips by emphasizing that the realities of parenting don't always allow us the luxury of following these techniques every time we are listening to our children. Many times parents are doing well if they are paying attention with one ear while multitasking all the other things that must get done. These tips are meant to enhance the listening experience for you *and* your child. If you commit to practicing them—and it will take commitment—you will get to know your child better, and your child will open up more in the welcoming environment you have provided.

Tip 1: Face Your Children and Maintain Eye Contact While They Are Speaking

Have you ever read tips for performing well in a work interview? The same rules apply with your children. Lean forward, with appropriate responsive gestures or comments that convey your interest. Slouching back with arms folded and looking bored will stifle the conversation.

Turning your body toward your children is a very strong nonverbal message that you are open to them and paying attention. It also means you aren't on the computer or texting at the same time. Remember how effective a turned head is—for encouraging or discouraging communication. And consider bringing yourself down to your kids' level. Don't tower over them when talking. Give them equal footing, literally.

Tip 2: When They Want to Talk, Be Sure You're Available

Usually the most important discussions don't follow a convenient timetable. I know two parents who made it a point to immediately turn off the television whenever one of their kids came in and wanted to talk. Think how good it made that child feel to know that they come first in the parents' world. That boost to your child's confidence should be worth the momentary parental sacrifice.

Also, cell phones are a wonderful thing. Children can now reach their parents at anytime and anyplace. There may need to be some ground rules, especially if the parent works, but a phone call or text can really bolster that bond.

Tip 3: Be Aware of Your Tone and Facial Expressions

Kids are hyper aware of reading their parents' cues, no matter how hard they pretend otherwise. If your children are taking the risk of sharing something heavy with you and they see you roll your eyes, sigh quietly, or even just say, "yes, yes" with the tightly controlled mouth grimace that indicates you are gearing up for a conflict, they are going to close down so quickly you won't even have a clue as to what just happened.

No matter what they share, don't act shocked or make a big deal out of it in the moment. If a child thinks the parent is going to go nuts and fly off the handle when they hear something, the child isn't ever going to take the risk of telling.

If you listen with eyebrows arched and eyes twinkling, you are in one move expressing to your teenager how much they mean to you—and you haven't uttered a word. Always remember: eye contact. Think back to the last time you were speaking to someone whose eyes were constantly breaking away and scanning the room. Wasn't it exasperating, trying to talk to someone when it felt like they were searching for someone else to talk to? Do you remember the feeling of irritation, inadequacy, embarrassment, or maybe even defiance that their feigned interest, or lack of interest, engendered in you? That is how it makes your children feel as well, but probably more so, given that their self-confidence is still developing.

Tip 4: Focus on What Your Child Is Saying

Don't get distracted by their messy hair or their baggy pants. Now isn't the time. Nor should you start formulating the speech you are going to give to solve their problem or set them straight. Listen to the spoken and unspoken message. Look at their body language as they speak to you. And definitely let go of your preconceived notions of "how" your child is saying something and what you believe they "should" be saying. Don't worry about the way they exaggerate or the language they use that you might not appreciate. Instead, start trying to understand "what" your child is saying. You're not listening to them to see whether they make sense to you; you're listening to try to see the world from their vantage point.

And, above all, remain quiet. Adolescents need to go for a while uninterrupted. If you just let them talk, they will move from a superficial, warm-up stage to a deeper, more intense level where their real feelings lie.

Tip 5: Try Very Hard Not to Get Defensive

Think of yourself as the trial attorney, or the interviewer, gathering information. Some of the hardest, yet most important, things for your children to talk to you about may come out as complaints or attacks. Immediately defending yourself will just drop everything into an adversarial back-and-forth. So, once again, keep quiet. Let your children fully express their feelings. Sometimes giving them the chance to express their frustration will release some of the tension.

Tip 6: Reflect Your Child's Feelings

After your child appears to have finished expressing himself, reflect, restate, and empathize with their feelings. Tell your child up front that you don't want to misinterpret what you think they mean.

Sometimes this step is very difficult. You want to erupt in judgments or solutions or critical analysis. Instead, hold back, and maintain your focus. When done correctly, this active reflection will help you clarify what your teenager said, avoid wasteful misunderstandings, and reassure your child that you understood what they were trying to communicate.

Tip 7: Remember, It Is Not About *You*

Let go of your emotions when your teenager is talking to you. If you're feeling anger, sadness, or any sort of anxiety, set it all aside. Harboring those emotions not only will dramatically distort what you think you are hearing, but will almost always cause you to respond in some self-serving or perhaps even inflammatory way.

And, please, never start regaling your children with stories about how that same thing also once happened to you but was "so much harder." If they ask for advice, sometimes a similar story is enlightening and comforting. But otherwise, keep the focus on them.

7

Talking to Your Children

Y ou have the listening techniques down. Now it is time to talk. You might think you have this one covered. Not so fast. Most parents spend their time talking *at* their children rather than talking *to* them. The truth is, most parents aren't communicating with their children very well. Why not? It all comes down to positive vs. negative.

I have a feeling that most parents have no idea how much "negative talk" they aim at their kids. Often, the reprimands, criticisms, and accusations come after a long day at the office. Without realizing it, by the end of the day parents' voices may be strained and tense, getting louder and louder as they try to deal with their children.

How, you might ask, did this happen? Just like you stopped listening to your kids, you become less attentive to how to talk to them. Here's the good news: Your bad talking habits are much easier to change than you might suspect. This chapter contains some key points for when you, the parent, have the floor.

■ Skip the Criticism

When anyone, much less an emotional child or a hormonal teenager, feels they are being criticized, they either shut down, withdraw, or attempt to get back at the person criticizing them. And in the end, your children hear and learn very little about what you were trying to tell them. All they remember is that you verbally attacked them, and it didn't feel good.

So, what good does it do for you to spend a 20-minute conversation criticizing your kids, adamantly telling them what they should or should not be doing? Why not spend that time subtly helping your children discover those lessons for themselves? Instead of grilling them, just get to the meat of your discussion.

At the core of every criticism, you'll likely discover a request. You want the other person to change in some way, but first you vent your frustration with a string of criticism. So, why not just skip the criticism and get right to the request at the heart of it? Amazing! That is much more productive and respectful than first unleashing a torrent of disparagement and condemnation.

Why would any child be eager to do whatever you're requesting if it's delivered in the form of criticism anyway? Let's say your son constantly drops all of his school stuff on the floor right in the middle of the hallway the moment he gets home. You have told him over and over to put his stuff away. Tonight you get home after a long day of work and practically fall over the pile of stuff blocking the hall. You see your son lounged in front of the TV on the couch. Sure, you could lambast him how you almost fell down, how exhausted you are, how lazy and selfish he is.... Once you get going, I'm sure the list could go for a while. But what is it that you truly want him to *do* and *learn*?

How about taking a deep breath, sitting down next to your son, putting the TV on pause, giving him a smile, and saying something like this, "Hey, bud! I just wanted to let you know that when I walk in the door at night and I see a clean hallway in front of me, it makes me smile. You know why? Because I know that you took the time and effort to think of me and then took the extra step to put your stuff in your bedroom. And when I see that message from you, it makes me happy." Then give him a moment to respond when he realizes that he left his stuff in the hallway again. If he apologizes, great. If he doesn't, keep the tone positive and say, "Maybe there is another place, besides the hallway or your room, that works for both of us. Or is there some way to help remind yourself right when you walk in?"

Do you see what I'm suggesting? If you feel a lecture coming on in which you want to tell your kids exactly how they failed, you should stop it before it starts. The best conversations between you and your teenagers are the ones where they never feel their backs are pushed against the wall. It's an actual "conversation." Instead of telling them how stupid they are for something they did, try to turn it around to how they can succeed. If they have done something stupid or wrong that triggers serious consequences, hold back on the "I warned you! How could you be so stupid?" lecture. Try to express sympathetic understanding for the fear and frustration they may be feeling over what they did and the ramifications they now must face. You can give them an arm's-length suggestion to show support, without releasing them of their responsibilities.

Here's another example: Let's say your daughter tells you she's going to fail an upcoming test in chemistry but she doesn't care because she hates the class anyway. You might be inclined to say, "I'm sacrificing a lot to get you the best education possible, and you better study right now or that's it!" or "Well, honey, you just need to study more." But you'll get further if you start a conversation that reflects her true feeling—something like "You're feeling pressured, huh?" Then move on to the true reason for the outburst and maybe: "I'm wondering if this is something that might work to help you feel more prepared for school...." Then offer up a piece of advice about studying.

By talking to them respectfully like adults, they're more likely to respond respectfully, like adults. You also provide choices for them to make mature decisions.

Instead of wasting time verbally releasing your own exasperation, which just distracts from your ultimate goal of parenting, you are putting the burden of responsibility squarely on your child's shoulders. A good go-to phrase like "Wow, that's a tough situation you've gotten into. What are you going to do to get things right?" will help them realize they have to deal with the consequences of what they've done, rather than spend time defending themselves to you. That kind of reaction builds self-control. The other kind just continues the parent control.

■ Pick the Time and Place to Talk

I can tell you with great certainty, if you are lecturing your child in public, you are wasting your breath. Your child will not hear a word you say because the rush of embarrassment and humiliation will drown out all other sounds.

There was a time when, as a criminal prosecutor, I had to go out and find a key witness who had failed to show up for court. I was in the middle of trial, and this witness was the ex-girlfriend of the defendant whom I was prosecuting for killing a police officer. She had a teenage son with the defendant. After court recessed for the day, I went with a police detective to the gang-infested neighborhood where my witness lived. Within minutes of parking at the curb, the relatively quiet street came alive. Whether it was the "undercover" dark blue Crown Vic we were driving, my suit and heels, or the telling lump under the detective's jacket where he had his holster strapped, we were attracting a lot of attention. Window curtains were fluttering. Front doors were opening. A variety of residents suddenly decided to step out into their front yards, leaning against their wire fences, watching us.

The detective and I made our way to the witness's apartment and knocked on the door. Not wanting her name to be broadcast, our witness opened the door, just a few inches. I started asking her why she didn't show up for court but stopped short when I caught a glimpse of her distraught, terrified face. I realized, belatedly, that there was absolutely no way my witness was hearing a word I said. She was too concerned with what all of her neighbors were thinking. And what her son was thinking, who, unbeknownst to me, was standing behind her and was adamant that she not testify against his father and perhaps put him on death row. I realized that my determination to talk to this witness had overshadowed what should have been my first consideration—is this the best time and place to speak with her? Obviously, it wasn't.

While the stakes aren't as life-threatening, our kids are also concerned about what their peers think about them. Lashing out at them, lecturing them, or waving the big "parental authority flag" in front of your child's peers will not lead to a worthwhile conversation.

Bite your tongue, hold your breath, and wait until you are alone with your child. Then you can both focus on the discussion, without distractions. And you have graciously allowed your child's dignity to remain intact. Your patience will pay off.

■ Know When to "Take Five"

If you can feel your child getting more and more frustrated during a conversation, then don't hesitate to take a break. It's perfectly fine to say "Let's continue this tomorrow." So often we stubbornly continue to push, even after a conversation has sunk into a verbal version of head-butting. Neither side is going to relent, but the heightened emotions can cause each side to make comments that can cause lasting damage. Step back. Let both sides breathe, reflect, and refocus.

And if your kid suddenly gets up during a talk and walks out in anger, please think twice before yelling, "Come back here, I'm talking to you!" What might be at work here is pride— either yours (your own desire to be heard) or your child's (wanting to regain some dignity). By this point, your kid has, no doubt, already heard what you have to say. And you could be so emotionally wound up that you're repeating yourself without realizing it. Don't "overkill" your message.

Do you find yourself always needing to "have the last word?" Let it go. That need comes from the urge to exercise "parent control." Insisting on ending every conversation with one great parental proclamation once again undermines your child's self-control, which both of you are trying to build up. Don't let foolish pride take that away.

■ The Lost Art of Praising Your Teenager

Words are like fire. They hold the power to do both amazing good and great destruction. We've touched on the destruction of criticism. Now I want to discuss the incredible power of words to encourage, support, and praise.

Remember the five-to-one communication ratio I discussed in the "The Punishing Parent" section? Knowing that it takes five positive comments to equal one negative comment should make all parents stop and consider before making even one negative comment! Parents should never risk underestimating the power of a negative comment or ignore how vital your positive interactions are for your children and for the health of your relationship.

Here's an exercise for you to try: For one day, keep a running tally of your interactions with your children, and rate each one as positive or negative. It will be interesting to see your overall ratio. Do it again the next day, and see whether you can raise your positive number and decrease your negative number. Many experienced dieters attribute their success to keeping a food diary—a running list of every item of food they consume each day. They say it forces them to be more aware of how much they are actually eating and gives them motivation to do better. So, put the philosophy to work in your parental-child relationship. I promise you, the higher the positive number goes up and the lower the negative number drops, the better your children will do.

Positive interactions can be as simple as these:

- "Hey, I like your outfit. You really have a great fashion sense."

- "You made your bed. Nice!"

- "When I got home from work and saw that you had set the table, it really made me happy. Thank you for being so thoughtful!"

- "I admire how kind you are to all of your friends, without taking sides or playing favorites."

- "Your smile this morning made my whole day."

Your teenagers need to be reminded how much you genuinely like them. And you need to point that out in specific ways. It might take a couple minutes for you to think of something positive. But those are the times your child needs to hear the positive comment the most. Even if you're having a discussion with them on how their grades have been slipping, for example, still make sure to point out your pride about the times they did excel in school or other things they're doing well.

Kids do better when they focus on their strengths, not fixate on their weaknesses. And they will thrive when they know they are admired. Perhaps you remember a time in your own youth when something was said to you by your parents or by another adult. Perhaps one of them looked at you and said in a completely uncontrived and sincere way, "What a neat kid you are. I love being around you." Do you remember how it made you feel? Words like that can make a struggling child feel like they can conquer the world.

That's what will happen with your own children if you use your words carefully. The right words can be an influential tool in building your child's confidence and identity.

And it's all because you learned how to talk to them.

■ Six Ways to Increase Your Child's Listening Pleasure

In the same way you want to present yourself as an empathetic listener, you also need to present yourself to your teenager in a way that makes them feel comfortable while you are speaking. Over the years, I interviewed hundreds of reluctant witnesses. Some were defiant, some were scared, while others were just overwhelmed and confused. But I found that they were all more open to what I had to say if I was sensitive to how I was presenting myself. If you are able to speak in a caring, concerned, and nonthreatening manner, your children will be able to relax and really *hear* what you are saying, rather than responding with a "fight or flight" mentality.

1. **Don't make big gestures when you talk.** Waving your hands in your child's face will make them want to retreat—physically and emotionally. Avoid pointing at your teenager too. It doesn't make you feel comfortable when someone does it to you, right? Show respect to get respect.

2. **Keep your voice low in pitch and calm.** It might be counterintuitive, but the louder you speak, the less your kid hears. Regardless of the words you are saying, raising your voice sounds like a call for conflict.

3. **Use short sentences.** The more time and air you use up rambling, the less time and air there will be left for a give-and-take discussion.

4. **Pace your speech.** Don't talk super-fast just because you feel you need to quickly respond to your child. And don't help them finish their sentences. Often, when your teenagers are talking, they will stop in mid-sentence, having lost their train of thought. Give them a moment rather than seizing on the silence. You must wait patiently. Even if they don't finish what they are trying to say until another conversation, they'll get there. Pushing the tempo reflects your need to control.

5. **Keep eye contact while you are speaking.** Focusing your attention on your listener emphasizes the importance of what you are saying.

6. **Do not repeat yourself.** It's very annoying. It's very annoying. It's very annoying. See? Your kids are smart, and even if they are pretending not to listen, they heard what you said the first time.

■ Creative Noncommunication Techniques

Sometimes the best way to communicate with your child is by a means other than just speech. Sending a nonverbal message often allows your teenagers to process the information at their own speed and from their own point of view. Here are some examples:

A mother and father were concerned about their young adult daughter's fiancé. It appeared to them that he was short on focus, had different values, and lacked a work ethic. But their daughter was head over heels in love with the guy, and they didn't want to alienate her if she was determined to marry him. Instead of saying anything, they invited the fiancé to come on the annual family vacation to Hawaii.

The whole family looked forward to this trip all year, and they were adamant about reenacting all the same activities, which now were essentially family traditions. During the trip, it became apparent that the fiancé wasn't embracing all the fun family activities. He spent most of his time lying on the couch while everyone else pitched in. When the family had their lively dinnertime discussions, the fiancé resisted efforts to draw him in. About three weeks after the trip, the parents received a call from their daughter, saying she had called off the wedding. She just didn't think he was the right one for her.

One mother felt strongly about no swearing in her home. Whenever her children had friends over and she heard one of them cussing, she would simply say, "Oh, I'm sorry. We don't allow swearing in our home. You'll need to go home now." Nothing more, nothing less. Both her children and their friends got the message right away, and they all began to self-regulate each other so they could continue hanging out at the house.

One mother wanted to emphasize the importance of being kind to others. She was a great baker and loved to bake for her family. Whenever she made something, she doubled the recipe. She would wrap up the second dessert and then have her children take it to a neighbor. The recipient was always surprised and delighted at the unexpected kindness. The children were able to see and feel the impact of their random act of generosity.

A father found out that his son was starting to hang out with a new group of friends who were known for spraying graffiti around town. He bought some paint and a huge artist's pad of paper. He then gave the supplies to his son and encouraged him to paint whatever he wanted. After looking at the finished product, he praised his artistic ability and offered to sign him up for art classes.

One middle-class couple wanted to teach their children the importance of helping others less fortunate than them and to appreciate all the good things they had in their lives. Every Christmas, starting when their children were young, they would use the money that would normally be spent on gifts and instead use it to go on a weeklong humanitarian trip to a third-world country. The entire family would work together doing manual service. They would get to know people with a different culture and language. And every year they came back to their home more bonded and appreciative than when they left.

Remember, no matter how great your message may be, it won't matter if your child doesn't hear it. Take the time to build consistent, respectful lines of communication with your children. Then, not only will they hear what you are teaching them, they will also know that they can turn to you for reasonable, compassionate counsel when they are in a crisis. And for children, that kind of reassurance is invaluable.

8

Better Kids Through Better Families

We sometimes try to make the raising of children a complicated science, yet we often forget that it is sometimes the smallest, simplest activities that can have enormous positive consequences. Here is a great example: family dinners, a time where parents and kids can talk freely and enjoy one another's company without any of the pressures of the outside world pushing in.

Are you chuckling at my naïveté? Well, guess what? In 2007, a study was conducted by The National Center on Addiction and Substance Abuse at Columbia University, which compared teens who ate dinner frequently with their families (at least five times per week) with teens who had infrequent family dinners (three or less per week). Those teens who had infrequent family dinners were:

- 3½ times likelier to have abused prescription drugs

- 3½ times likelier to have used an illegal drug other than marijuana or prescription drugs

- 3 times likelier to have used marijuana

- 2½ times likelier to have used tobacco

- 1½ times likelier to have used alcohol

You can't just chalk that up to coincidence, can you?

Yes, I know it may sound simplistic when I say better families build better kids. But in our busy, distracted lives we sometimes overlook this fundamental truth. If you want to build your children's self-esteem, keep them on the path to success, and prevent them from the temptations of peer pressure and other outside influences, the best place to do it is within a strong family. In fact, of all the tasks I have asked you to do so far in this book, there might be nothing more important than you creating that happy home.

Many of the young people I met in court who were making poor choices didn't feel a strong connection to their parents or family. The ones who were emotionally twisted up in knots often came from a family environment that was also twisted up in knots. They were looking elsewhere to find that bond and attention, whether it was turning to drugs and alcohol, getting involved in inappropriate or destructive relationships, committing crimes, or even running away from home.

Life at Home

They say the home is a man's castle. I, on the other hand, have always said my home is a safe haven. Every day we go out into a world where we face failure and rejection. During my years as a single mother to my son, I worked hard to make our home a place where we could retreat, away from conflict, and feel safe. If your children know that home is a place where people will have your back, they will want to be there.

And surprisingly, the biggest advocates for these kinds of changes just might be your kids. Your children want a good family life. Remember that study I mentioned before, about the importance of family dinner? In that same study, 84 percent of the teens surveyed said they would *prefer* to eat dinner with their family. Can you imagine? A time when your kids actually want to be with you?

So, let's start there.

13 Steps to Build a Better Family

1. **Eat together.** Make it a priority to schedule at least four to five dinners a week together as a family. In addition to all the important factors mentioned, data gathered by Rutgers University shows that kids who eat dinner with their family at least three times a week are less depressed, eat healthier food, and are more likely to say that they have a supportive family and are happy at home.

2. **Establish a regular "family night."** Besides the family dinner, I think it's important to pick one night of the week where everyone, including Mom and Dad, keep their calendars clear

for family time. Set aside an hour or two. Start with a mini family meeting. The agenda should cover the week's calendar so everyone knows the schedule for lessons, birthdays, special events, and so forth. There should also be time allotted to discuss any family issues, like gripes between the siblings or problems with the family rules. Parents listen and come up with solutions that utilize the children's input. If there is a tense issue to discuss, you can institute the "five-minute rule." Each member of the family gets to talk about the issue for five minutes, and there can be no interruptions, no harrumphs, no eye rolls—nothing but sincere listening by the rest of the members of the family until it is their turn to talk. Then get to the family fun time—a movie, a favorite television show, hide-and-seek, or a board game. Rotate which family member gets to choose the "fun" event for that week. But the key is that everyone must participate. And always, always, always have a yummy, easy dessert as the finale of the evening.

3. **Build a family identity.** My parents were always very firm about putting out a unified front. They would tell us, "We may fight among ourselves at home, but once we step outside, we have each other's backs." As a result, we supported each other, never badmouthing each other in public. When possible, we attended each other's sporting events and concerts. We were "family." It gave us a sense of belonging, and to this day, we know that no matter what happens, we are here for one another. I'll never forget my first day riding the bus to a new school when I was five. I was so scared, but my older brother, who loved to tease me mercilessly around the house, saw my fear and sat next to me the whole time— even after we were told by the other kids that the boys all sat on the other side of the bus. Even at the age of nine,

my brother had learned to put family before the ridicule of other kids.

4. **Schedule family service projects.** This is a great activity to build family unity. Volunteering as a family can go a long way in teaching your children empathy for others. It shows your kids ways they can make a difference. And it builds their understanding of gratitude.

   I know a mother and father who committed to spending one Saturday a month doing volunteer work together with their children. When the kids were young, they would find some age-appropriate service project that they could all do together. It became a family habit. Now that the kids are older, they get to pick the projects themselves. It could be volunteering at an animal shelter or a soup kitchen. Or the entire family could do a major trash pickup together in their own neighborhood.

5. **Laugh together.** Laughter is a great way, especially when things get heavy, to step back, take a moment to look at the big picture, and remind each other that no matter how bad it is, it will be okay. You will get through it together. Humor can deflect fear and recrimination. It helps connect you with your children. How many times have you heard your kids laughing at some stupid cat video on YouTube? Take the time to watch and laugh along with them. Just be careful to make sure that the laughter is never at the expense of others.

6. **Create one-on-one parent-child time.** Once a month, plan a one-on-one with each child. Make it something easy, like going for a walk or grabbing a bite to eat. Let the child dictate the topic of conversation, whether it is serious or light and

frivolous. You are showing the child that their thoughts and words are important and interesting to you. If the child doesn't seem to know what to talk about, have some fun, nonthreatening conversation starters ready. For example, try asking your child what is the biggest thing they are dreading to have to do that week, who their favorite artist is, what they would like to do in that given month, or what their favorite teacher does that makes him or her so good. Don't press going too deep or serious if your child doesn't seem interested. The goal is to let them know you are ready to listen but that just spending time together, without "accomplishing" anything, is great, too.

7. **Never play favorites.** Let's face it—there is going to be a child or two who you personally relate to better than the others. But parents of multiple children must be acutely aware of not showing overt favoritism among the children. It causes turmoil, resentment, and lifelong grudges. As adults, my six siblings and I joke about "the list": which one of us is Mom's favorite child at that moment in time, ranking down to who is currently in the doghouse. Mom fails to see the humor in it, because she is so sensitive to not wanting to play favorites. However, *because* Mom did such a good job making each one of us feel loved, we actually find great humor in it. And no matter where we might fall on the imaginary "list," we are secure in knowing that Mom will still love us.

8. **Build traditions.** Traditions don't have to be fancy or expensive. A favorite cookie recipe. An annual drive up the canyons to see the fall colors. When I was growing up, Christmas Eve always included mom telling our favorite Christmas stories

by the tree. Then we would act out the nativity story in our bathrobes.

A young husband and father told me that when he was growing up, his whole family would spend July 4th at the same beach every year, playing in the waves, and building sand castles. They would have sandwiches and chips for lunch, and for dinner they would grill hamburgers and make s'mores. The fireworks that shot out over the water were his favorite part. It was such a great memory for him that now he wants to replicate it for his own children.

9. **Establish family mottoes.** Family mottoes are not only fun, they can help ground your family identity. They can be as simple as, "We are Andersons, and Andersons don't lie." There is a nice ring to it, and your little children can remember it and repeat it easily. Here's another one I've heard a family use: "It's nice to be important, but it's more important to be nice. We, the Clarks, are nice."

My dad's motto for our family was, "The appreciation of diversity is the basis of unity." No, it didn't really roll off the tongue, but it was a good reminder for me and my siblings. Growing up in a family of seven adopted children from different ethnic backgrounds, I think my parents did an extraordinary job of making us all feel proud of our differences while simultaneously feeling very connected together.

10. **Share your values.** We have already talked about building your children's values as one of the cornerstones of their mental-moral core. As a family, you should build up a core of shared values—principles that you strive for together. One of the ways to enhance your family's commitment to these

values is to join a larger community that shares your values. A social or religious group that espouses values similar to your family values can provide your family with the comfort and strength of a supportive community.

11. **Serve each other**. Teach your children to help and serve each other. When you are helping someone else, warm feelings develop for both the giver and the receiver. The competitive tendency among many siblings will hold less allure as the focus on teamwork grows.

    Make it into a game with your children. Pull names for "secret sibling" surprises. For a week, each child thinks of nice things to do anonymously for the named sibling. While they are thinking of nice things to do for that other child, they are having nice things done for them. A made bed, a favorite candy bar slipped into a drawer, even a smiley face note tucked into their lunch. The children learn that giving to each other feels as good as receiving.

12. **Smile and hug.** It is amazing how far a smile goes in conveying love and care to another person. Why not do it for your own family? Smiling is such an easy gesture. And yet, it might be the only friendly face your child sees that day. My father was not overly physical with his kids. But one day he heard another father whom he admired say that he never walked by one of his children without giving them a little physical touch, whether it be a pat on the arm or a squeeze of the shoulder. It was his way of reminding his children that he was there for them and loved them. After that, my dad worked on doing this for his kids. It didn't come naturally to him, but he got better at it over time. And to this day, one of my favorite memories

with my dad is a hug he gave me during an ominous lightning storm. I don't think I ever felt as safe as I did that night.

13. **Know when to seek outside assistance.** Parents who refuse to admit their family may need expert help because they don't want to tarnish their "perfect family" image are sacrificing the health and well-being of their loved ones for the fleeting perceptions of outsiders. Many families will go through a crisis at one point or another when they could greatly benefit from some objective outside eyes.

Parenting Notes

Parenting Notes

Parenting Notes

Part 3

The Danger Zones:
How to Protect Your Child from the Outside

Dealing with Drugs and Alcohol

When they want to get high, today's kids are more resourceful than ever. No longer applicable is the stereotype of the "druggies and stoners"—the disheveled, gray-toned motley crew that congregates at the back fence of the schoolyard, smoking the joints they bought from their shady dealer. Today's kids don't have to venture into the "seedy" part of town to score their drugs. Now, all they have to do is open their parents' medicine cabinet or wine cabinet, sneak a few of their little brother's ADHD pills, or go into the garage and sniff some glue. They can go on the Internet and find the recipe for how to make methamphetamine or pretty much any other drug they are curious to try.

One of the fastest ways for your kids to end up in front of a criminal prosecutor is to be involved with drugs. Your child's use of drugs isn't just a health and addiction issue; it's a very fast path to jail. Many of the cases you read about in the newspaper or hear about on television are committed by someone either who is under the influence of drugs or who is so desperate to feel that intoxicating high that they will do anything to get it, including committing crimes.

When I talk about drugs, I'm including alcohol and prescription pills, whether they have been obtained legally or not. The mind-altering, physically impairing qualities of these and the other more readily recognized "bad" drugs have ended more innocent young lives than you could probably imagine.

■ What Kind of Problem You're Facing

The teenage years are the absolute most dangerous time for your child to try drugs or smoking or alcohol. Why? It has to do with the adolescent brain. Honestly, the way the brain develops makes your job as a parent that much harder. The human brain starts maturing in the back and works its way to the front. Unfortunately, the "prefrontal cortex," which governs things like inhibiting inappropriate or risky behavior and making good judgments, doesn't fully mature until around the age of 25. Add to that the fairly new discovery that during the teenage years, the brain actually starts to weed out extra synapses. Dr. Jay Giedd refers to this as the "use it or lose it" principle, because the behaviors that your child is practicing during their teenage years, whether it be studying, playing sports, watching TV, or doing drugs or drinking alcohol, are the parts of the brain that stay, while the unused parts get pruned out.

That combination of factors going on in your teenager's brain makes these years the danger zone for substance abuse. That is why your teenager may start acting more impulsive and taking more risks, including experimenting with drugs and alcohol. At the same time, the brain is vulnerable to repeated behaviors, so the impact "sticks," and by adulthood it is hard-wired in the brain.

Thus, if your child starts drinking by the age of 13, they have a 43 percent chance of becoming an alcoholic. If you can get them to hold off trying alcohol until the age of 21, you greatly increase their chances of not becoming addicted, because the number drops dramatically to 10 percent.

It's estimated that about 75 percent of all high-school students have tried some sort of addictive drug and that one in five are medically addicted. And before you assume that your child is in that 25 percent that would never use drugs, much less consider getting involved in drugs, let me open your mind to why they just might.

5 Reasons Why Your Child May Decide to Use Drugs

1. **Social benefits.** Kids want to be accepted, especially kids who struggle with self-esteem. Socializing and fitting in can be much less awkward for your kids if they and those around them are high. Ecstasy, the popular "love drug," does a great job at making everyone feel loved and connected.

2. **Form of escape.** Just like adults, drugs are a way for kids to self-medicate. Overwhelmed by painful feelings of insecurity, doubt, or depression? Drugs can mask those feelings with a fake high. Escaping into drugs can seem easier than facing the challenges of growing up.

3. **Enables higher achievements.** Don't think that your teenagers haven't noticed how many professional athletes are competing with the aid of drugs. A teen under pressure to excel

in sports and grades could look to a variety of amphetamines to keep going. Sometimes they are encouraged to do so by their coaches. Even energy drinks like Red Bull can be addicting and lead to a need for even stronger drugs to provide a bigger boost. Colleges are now dealing with the rampant use of "smart pills"—illegally obtained prescription drugs like Adderall and Ritalin that enhance the cognitive functioning of already high-functioning Type A personalities. These drugs are easily purchased at some universities from student dealers, selling surreptitiously out of their dorm rooms.

4. **Experimentation.** Teenagers like to seek out adventure. (Just think about why movies like *Jackass* are so popular among teenagers.) Thus, it's the nature of being a teenager to try something mood-altering. Being "under the influence" of alcohol or drugs gives kids the freedom to be "wild" and then blame it on the drugs/alcohol later. And this is in addition to the brain development issue we just discussed.

5. **You.** The biggest reason of all for your child to use may be, ironically, you, the parent. When you think about it, it becomes pretty obvious, right? If you're not setting a drug-free example in your own life, then you are encouraging your child to try drugs too. If you use socially in front of your children, you are showing them by example that it is perfectly okay for them to use. If you drink alcohol to celebrate or to make you feel better at the end of a bad day, then your kids will get the message. They'll get the message about drinking and driving if they see you erratically pull into the driveway after having gone out for a few drinks. If you have drugs or alcohol in the house, you are making them easily accessible for your children to use. At some point, your kids will decide that if it is okay for Mom and Dad, then it must be okay for them.

What You Can Do: Stop Using

The best thing you can do for your own kids is to start cutting drugs and alcohol out of your own life. Before you roll your eyes and harrumph in disgust, ask yourself this question—what stronger influence is there on a child than the modeling of their parents? Trying to teach your children to do something you aren't doing yourself is like swimming upstream. If you can't commit to cutting out drugs and alcohol altogether, then at least commit to using them in a responsible manner. Remember, you are a parent. You need to be your best self for the sake of your children.

Talk to Your Kids!

A study from the Partnership for a Drug-Free America found that when parents of high-school teens talked to their kids about a "zero tolerance" for drugs and alcohol at prom or graduation, only 16 percent of the teens reported the likelihood of using, whereas 45 percent of the teens whose parents didn't talk to them reported that they were likely to use. Talking to your kids about drugs sounds obvious, but amazingly, according to the teenagers, only about 31 percent of the parents are doing it. Whether your kids appear to be or not, they *are* listening. And when you teach them about the risks, your child is 50 percent less likely to use than their peers. So, speak up!

Get Informed

Show your teenager you are educated about drugs and their impact. When it comes to drugs, teenagers think their parents are seriously out of touch. They have a point. Since you were teenagers, a lot of new drugs and new methods for getting high from ingredients easily purchased at your local drug store have hit the streets. And all the information and instructions are just a Google click away.

You need to know what your kids are tempted to use. What are the latest, crazy ways teens are creating to get high? Bath salts? Nutmeg? Prescription-strength cough syrup? It is important to educate yourself and be ready to talk about how damaging those drugs are. I've heard of kids trying to persuade their parents that LSD is not harmful. That's what you're facing these days. You need to be more informed than they are.

■ Understand the Risks of the "One Time Won't Hurt" Mentality

Many parents figure that when it comes to drugs and alcohol, "one time won't hurt." You know, kids want to experiment; it isn't that big of a deal. Right? Wrong.

Based on fairly recent scientific discoveries regarding our genetic makeup, *one time* may be enough to hook your child for the rest of his or her life. Geneticists have determined that people with certain genes are more susceptible to addiction. In fact, a person's genes account for 50 percent of their vulnerability to addiction. (The other half is environment.) For those with a predisposed genetic makeup, it is harder to quit once they have tried a drug, legal or illegal, or tobacco or alcohol. They may experience more severe withdrawal symptoms if they try to quit. On the flip side, someone else's genetic makeup might cause them to feel sick when they try a drug, thus inhibiting them from any further desire.

But here is the catch: Which one is your child? If you don't know your child's genetic composition—and most of us don't—allowing that "one time" is like playing Russian Roulette with your child's future. Do you want to take that risk?

Let me give you one more piece of information to help you in your evaluation of whether it's okay for your child to have a glass of wine at the holidays or to try beer at the big party this weekend or to puff on a "harmless" marijuana cigarette. Roughly 10 percent of all people who experiment with drugs become addicted.

Look at your child and nine of your child's friends. If they all experimented with some type of addictive substance, one of them is going to live the rest of their life struggling to not lose their identity, their dreams, and their future—all because they decided to try it "just once."

Use Scare Tactics

Many anti-drug campaigns resort to scare tactics, showing what drugs may do to your brain or how you might get into legal trouble. The research is inconclusive on whether this approach is effective. However, I stumbled inadvertently onto a scare tactic that made a big impression.

During my years as a prosecutor, I would often bring work home with me. One evening, I had a case file spread out over the coffee table. A friend stopped by to pick something up from me. She had her pre-teenage daughter with her. The girl's attention was riveted on two photos that were among the scattered papers. One showed a beautiful woman in her early 20s, with long flowing blond hair, rosy cheeks, and a lovely smile. The other photo, taken against the unflattering blue background used by the Sheriff's Department for standard mug shots, caught the image of a gaunt, sunken-eyed, hollow-cheeked woman with stringy hair and dead eyes. She looked like she was in her 50s.

My friend's sweet young daughter wanted to know who the women were. I explained that they were the same person.

The first was the driver's license photo of the woman, who was indeed in her early 20s. The second photo was a booking photo that had been taken nine months later, after she had been hooked on methamphetamine.

My young friend, who was just entering junior high—a world preoccupied with having the perfect body, the blemish-free face, the trendy wardrobe—was mesmerized at the shocking physical change. She peppered me with questions about what the young woman had done, what the drug was, and what was going to happen to her now. The drastic degradation of physical beauty may be one scare tactic that might work on young girls.

Watch Their Peers

Children rarely, if ever, decide to start using drugs on their own. They are usually introduced to the world of drugs by someone else—and it is usually a peer. Studies show that one of the biggest determiners in whether your child will use drugs is whether their peers use drugs. If their peers aren't using drugs, the chances are your kid isn't either.

Tell your kids this when they are choosing friends. And keep an eye on signs that their friends may be using. If you think they are, it is red-alert time for your children!

Teach Your Child How to Say "No"

Sometimes for your child, being able to do the right thing comes down to just knowing how to say "no." Brainstorm and role-play with your kids about different scenarios where they might be invited, or pressured, to drink or take drugs.

- *You are at a party and someone offers you a joint.*

- *Your friend is celebrating her birthday, and her mom is giving everyone champagne.*

- *Your boyfriend or girlfriend wants to get high together to "feel closer."*

Come up with ways that they can comfortably say "no" and withdraw from the situation. Good choices often come from planning ahead.

Drinking and Driving

Having prosecuted DUI cases for years, this is one issue that I cannot emphasize forcefully enough. Parents, you must impress upon your children, without equivocation, that under no circumstance should they ever drive after drinking. Tell your kids that you will *always* come get them if they have been drinking. No matter how upset you may be if they drink, they will always get points in your book if they call you for a ride home.

Explain to your children that if they get into a car to drive after drinking, their choice to drink has just expanded from impacting only their own future to impacting the future of every other person who is sharing the road with them. The possible downsides of drinking just jumped from waking up with a bad hangover to ending up in prison for the rest of your life, dealing with the guilt of having killed someone.

Some parents worry that if they talk about giving their child a ride home after drinking, somehow they are condoning or encouraging their kids to drink. Is it possible that providing a way home will be a factor that pushes them into drinking? Sure, anything is possible. However, the slight risk that comes with you offering the ride home is vastly outweighed by the deadly risk your child will take if they drink and then drive. And, while we're on the subject, make sure your children understand the equally deadly risk they are taking if they ride in a car with someone who has been drinking.

■ Assemble Your Crisis Management Plan Now

What are you going to do if you suspect your child is using drugs or alcohol? Decide ahead of time where you stand. How far are you willing to go to keep your kids off drugs? Will you institute random drug testing with a kit that you can get at a drug store? Put them in some out-patient rehab program the minute you discover they are using? Send them to an in-patient treatment facility for four to six weeks? Or let them get arrested?

These are tough decisions, but you need to think them through now. The earlier you establish a plan, the better. And then you need to be very clear with your kids about what you will do if you catch them with drugs. Those consequences should be ringing in their ears while they are weighing the pros and cons of taking that drug that is being offered to them.

And finally, you have to stick with it. If your kids sense for even a minute that you're wavering, then they aren't going to see your plan as a deterrent.

■ A Funeral to Remember

If you have seen or experienced addiction up close, you know you would do anything to keep your child from even the possibility, much less a one-in-ten chance, of that lifelong sentence.

A few years back, I attended a funeral of a young man. Halfway through the service, his mother made her way to the front of the congregation. Looking exhausted but determined, she started her speech by asking for everyone younger than 14 years old to leave the chapel. Then, in a clear voice, she shared what had happened to her son. In his early 20s, he had suffered a serious sports injury. He had started taking prescription medication to manage the pain. Soon, that just wasn't enough. He started self-medicating far beyond what the doctor had prescribed. His addiction grew, taking over his life. Eventually he began committing crimes to obtain more drugs. While it was hard for the mother to imagine, much less accept, that her son could possibly have a problem like this, she finally faced the reality. But before she was able to do anything, it was too late. Her son died from an unintentional overdose of the pain meds combined with alcohol and cold medication.

Sadly, since that funeral, I have heard this same scenario with increasing frequency—young people with great promise unintentionally getting ensnared by prescription drugs. Sometimes, their addictions led to death, while others have continued to struggle every minute of every day for the rest of their lives. Addiction is an insidious game-changer that no one expects. And we need to do everything we can to protect our children from it.

Assessing Your Child's Level of Risk

The following six questions can help you assess your own child—each "yes" answer increases their level of risk for using drugs.

1. Does your child have friends who use drugs or addictive substances?

2. Does your child lack affirmation or rewards from his or her social environment?

3. Is your child struggling academically?

4. Is there upheaval in your home from transitions or moving? Is there conflict in your family? (Divorce alone doesn't increase the risk, but family conflict does.)

5. Is there addiction in your family tree?

6. Do you use drugs, legal or illegal? Do you have drugs, legal or illegal, in your home?

10

The Perils of Technology

In my opinion, technology has really influenced this generation above anything else. In 1950, only 10 percent of American homes had a TV. Today, 99 percent of homes have TVs. Kids now watch approximately 28 hours of TV a week, which is more time than they spend in school. (More than half of all kids have a TV in their bedroom.) And when you add the radio, movies, and, of course, the Internet, the statistics are staggering. One 2010 study by the Kaiser Family Foundation found that teenagers spend in excess of 75 hours a week accessing "entertainment media."

The fact is that none of us is raising our children "tech-free." Whether it is a cell phone, a laptop computer, an iPad, or a flat-screen TV, our kids are surrounded by media gadgets. The psychologists who study these things have given our media-savvy children some cool monikers: "digital natives," "the net generation," "screenagers." And parents today are more than obliging to introduce their children to the joys and benefits of media technology at a very young age. Babies are plopped in front of the cartoons so Mom or Dad can get a break for a few minutes...or hours. By the time the child is 2 or 3 years old, they can tell you who is their favorite cartoon character and show you how to pull up their latest game app. I have seen kids as young as 2 entertaining themselves in a long church meeting with a video on their parent's iPad. Parents justify this wonderfully free babysitter as harmless at worst and potentially educational at best. It is easy, accessible, and rarely rejected by kids of all ages. And pretty much every parent does it, so it must be okay, right?

But have you ever thought about what you are freely exposing your children to on a daily basis? What exactly are you entrusting your kids *to*? I think you might get sick to your stomach when you read some of the following statistics about what impact modern-day entertainment media has on our children, particularly in the areas of sex and violence.

■ Sex

Young teens—ages 13 to 15—rank entertainment media as the top source of information about sexuality, sexual health, and sex education.

In a single year, a teenager will see roughly 14,000 references to sex on television. Only a fraction of those make any reference whatsoever to abstinence, birth control, risk of pregnancy, or sexually transmitted diseases.

Forty-seven percent of the female characters shown on television participating in sexualized depictions are underage, compared to adult females at 29 percent.

And if teens want to learn more about sex, they have the Internet right at their fingertips. One study found about

42 percent of teens and preteens view online porn, either deliberately or accidentally. A 2002 survey conducted by the London School of Economics actually found the number of children who had viewed pornography on the Internet to be much higher, around 90 percent. And is the porn showing couples in a committed, loving relationship? I think you already know the answer to that question. Children who watch porn are filling their developing brains with depictions of sex that focus on aggression, power, violence, and using women as sex objects. One survey reported that 54 percent of the young men found pornography to be "inspiring."

■ Violence

Before the age of 18, a typical American child views more than 200,000 acts of violence on television, including more than 16,000 murders. As much as we talk about prime-time violence, the level of violence in Saturday morning cartoons is actually higher: There are 3 to 5 violent acts per prime time hour versus 20 to 25 acts per cartoon hour.

On TV, perpetrators of violent acts go unpunished 73 percent of the time. On top of that, 58 percent of all violent interactions on TV don't show the victims enduring any pain. In other words, for a kid watching television, violent crime is not that big of a deal.

If you've been wondering why your sweet young child is becoming aggressive, anti-social, or impatient, perhaps you should take a look at what they are watching.

Hundreds of studies have shown a causal connection between media violence and aggressive behavior in some children. The more "real-life" violence portrayed, the greater likelihood it will be "learned."

Media violence is especially damaging to young children (younger than 8) because they cannot easily distinguish between real life and fantasy.

Media violence still influences teenagers. A 17-year study concluded that teens who watched more than one hour of TV a day were almost four times likelier than other teens to commit aggressive acts in adulthood.

A study of preschool children done at Pennsylvania State University revealed that after watching violent shows, the children were more likely to strike out at playmates, argue, and disobey authority.

Children who watch violent shows are less willing to wait for things.

◼ Impact on the Brain and Body

Still not concerned enough to take action? Well, this should motivate every parent to reassess their children's use of technology. An American Academy of Pediatrics study shows that TV and video games may "impoverish" the development of the part of the brain that manages self-control and moral judgment.

Television viewing has been proven to be a significant factor in childhood obesity. Studies also show that children who watch TV characters smoke and drink have a higher chance of picking up these habits themselves.

And the research indicates television viewing is an addictive habit. *Scientific American* reported that the moment viewers started watching TV they felt relaxed, but afterward, they felt let down.

Speaking of addictions, a study by the Chicago University's Business School found that social networks (like Twitter and Facebook) are potentially more addictive than cigarettes or alcohol.

If you think your child isn't addicted to their social networks, try cutting off their access to the computer and phone for one week. Watch for signs of headaches, anxiety, restlessness, irritability, an inability to concentrate, and depression. These are all classic signs of withdrawal.

■ Turning Everything Off

When I was in junior high, our old black-and-white television died. Rather than get it fixed, my parents decided to try life without TV. As it was, we had never really been a big TV-watching family. Sunday nights were grilled-cheese sandwiches in front of *The Mutual of Omaha's Wild Kingdom* and Walt Disney. Once in a while, if I sneaked out of bed, I would see my parents watching *The Bob Newhart Show*.

Still, we found ourselves going through a TV withdrawal, and it took a while for us to reassimilate. Eventually, we kids came up with a fun new activity for Sunday nights: shooting at each other with rubber bands while crawling silently around in a pitch-black living room. Then came the first crisis: *Gone with the Wind* was going to be broadcast in prime time. It was the talk of the school, and I begged my mother to let me watch. She held firm, saying she wasn't going to get the TV fixed just for that. Instead, she took me to the library, and we checked out the 500-page book. I hauled that huge thing around with me for a week and loved reading every page of it.

All that reading instilled a lifelong love affair with books for me and my brother and sister. We would ride our bikes to the library every Saturday and fill our bike baskets until they couldn't hold another book. We would spend hours, hiding somewhere, with a book and an apple (which my mother always said was the perfect accompaniment to a good book). At night we would sneak flashlights under the covers and read until we got caught. It gave us all great vocabularies, something that put us ahead later on aptitude tests and college admission exams.

I know times have really changed. Can you imagine a kid riding his bike to the library on a Saturday? Or a parent not just turning off the television and computers but taking them out of the house completely?

All right, I'm not naïve, and I know it's impossible to return children to the 1970s. I also know parents tend to panic over their children obsessively surfing the Internet or texting day and night. The truth is that most teenagers use the Internet and their cell phones the way previous generations flocked to the hamburger drive-in stands. These are places where kids can hang out and connect without adult interference.

Nevertheless, it would behoove all parents to set some guidelines. Block off certain times during the day when the TV and computer cannot be used. What's more, if you feel your teenagers are truly addicted to the television and their other high-tech gizmos, staying up way past a normal bedtime hour to engage in their activities, then it is imperative that you step in and restrict use, literally taking away the computer or television.

For the protection and safety of your children, one hard-and-fast rule every expert will tell you is to keep the computer in a public area of the house. No child should be allowed to take a laptop back to a corner of the house where no one can look over their shoulder. And if your child does happen to quickly minimize some window on the computer when you happen to walk by, then that is a sign you *must* investigate. You have to suspect something is happening online that your kid doesn't want you to know.

Go through the list of friends on your child's social networking sights. Ask who they are and how your child got to know them. Watch what photos they post and what they write.

You can snoop around and check their "search" history and see what websites they are hitting. If necessary, change the password to your Internet service provider until you are certain you know what is happening.

The Internet is filled with sexual predators and cyberbullies who are continually finding creative ways to connect with vulnerable young targets. Don't let your naïveté put your child at risk. Educate yourself and your children about potential dangers. Do the random checks. Let your children know that you will be involved in their Internet use. Know who is talking to your children online and what they are saying. It is up to you to make sure your children aren't inviting danger into your home.

11

What to Do About Sex

Sex. This isn't any parent's favorite topic, but no parent can afford to bury their head in the sand about it. Kids of this generation are growing up in a culture that relentlessly pushes the message that everyone has casual sex. Family sitcoms are filled with good-looking adults trying to have sex, having sex, or talking about the sex they just had. Moms are heading off to book club to talk about the thrill they get from the explicitly erotic *Fifty Shades of Grey* trilogy. We're raising our kids in a world that has emphasized sex to an unprecedented level, and if you sometimes feel like your personal messages to your children about the value of sex are drowned out by the noise of popular culture, I can't blame you. When your children have heard the debate of whether oral sex counts as "sex" from no less than a sitting U.S. President, it is tough to maintain some semblance of control over the sex issue.

Here is the good news: According to the latest studies conducted on sexual behavior in America, the percentage of teens having sex has stayed steady and has perhaps even dropped a bit. The 2010 U.S. National Center for Health Statistics report, which is based on data gathered in the 2006 to 2008 National Survey of Family Growth, found the percentage of girls between the ages of 15 and 19 who have had sex at least once just above 42 percent. For boys the same age, the number was 43 percent. And the number of teenagers deciding to wait has increased; 58 percent of teenage girls from ages 15 to 17 reported never having had a sexual contact. The percentage drops down for the 18- to 19-year-old girls to 28 percent. As for the boys from 15 to 17, 46 percent reported no sexual contact, with a drop to 22 percent for the 18 to 19 age bracket. Compared to the last data collected in 2002, this is about a 22 percent jump for the girls and an 8 percent increase for the boys.

However, it also appears that oral sex has become an integral part of our teenagers' sexual activity. According to a study done by the Centers for Disease Control and Prevention, which puts the percentages of teenagers ages 15 to 19 having intercourse at 44 percent for boys and 47 percent for girls, that same age group reported similar numbers for oral sex—49 percent for the boys and 48 percent for the girls. And overall, a quarter of the teens were found to be having oral sex before vaginal sex.

Another modern-day wrinkle is the prevalence of "sexting"—sending sexually explicit texts or photos. No longer is it just the politicians (Anthony Weiner) or professional athletes (Tiger Woods) engaging in this new form of entertainment. According to a new survey released by the *Journal of Pediatrics*, one out of seven Los Angeles high-school students who own a cell phone has sexted either a sexual photo of themselves or a sexually explicit text. And in a similar study done with Texas high-school students, about 57 percent of the teenagers reported having been asked to sext, while 28 percent reported having actually done it. And the studies showed that those teens who were sexting were more likely to be having sex. For all you parents with daughters, here is something you need to pay close attention to: The girls who had sent sexually explicit photos of themselves were more likely to engage in risky sexual behavior, such as multiple sexual partners, and using drugs or alcohol before sexual encounters.

I know we parents tend to have debates on whether teenagers *should* have sex. You can come up with a book full of reasons why sex isn't a good idea for teenagers, from their lack of emotional understanding to, for some, the immorality of premarital sex. But when you have about a 50/50 chance that your teen is about to, or already is, engaging in some type of sexual behavior, it is clearly time to step up and do more than just debate the issue.

The Sex Talk

So, what do you do? Throw up your hands and hope for the best? Actually, you can make a significant difference in how your teenagers approach sex by the way you talk to them about sex. No matter how much information about sex your kids are getting from other sources—and no matter what they are doing behind your back—they are unable in any rational, mature way to process what is happening to them. They might know all the words or sexual innuendos to describe various sexual functions (and, yes, they know those words at a stunningly early age), but they still have no idea what most of it *means*. Sadly, for many teens, sex is just something to do: There's little emotional connection, let alone any real passion, involved in the act. And for many others—perhaps your child—it's incredibly tantalizing and just as frightening, setting off a wildly confusing panoply of emotions.

Your children could use someone to provide wise, compassionate, but nonjudgmental counsel. I'm talking, of course, about you. First accept the fact that the "sex talk" you have with your kids will need to be different from the one you were probably given by your parents. The level of our children's sexual exposure and awareness, regardless of how much they actually understand, requires a more detailed, blunt approach than our parents took.

The "sex talk" should actually be a series of "sex talks"—an ongoing, evolving discussion that takes years. The talks should start when your children are very young, as you begin to teach them about their own bodies, referencing their private parts during potty training. That is a natural time to give simple explanations of their private parts and how they may be different from their friends of the opposite sex. Even at this young age, they can pick up on your own attitudes about certain body parts. Are they learning that their intimate areas are embarrassing and shameful? Or are they learning that they are important parts of our strong bodies and should be treated with special care?

When they reach the age of 4 to 6, you can have a short, simple talk about where babies come from, perhaps describing some details of the male and female genitalia. Most of it will not sink in. However, make sure to also talk about the emotional side of having a baby, so they can understand that it is more than just a physical act depicted on a diagram.

Then, when they hit early adolescence, you must always reassure them that they can ask you questions about sex and you will answer them as best you can. If something comes up at school (a classmate gets pregnant) or in a popular movie (everyone is talking about the "masturbation" scene), talk to them about it. Use it as an opening to gauge where they are as far as interest level and their own activity level.

And pay attention to your teenagers' own level of maturity and interest. If they have initiated a sex conversation with you, then that's your sign for a major talk—before they seek out the answers to their questions somewhere else.

Know What You Want to Say

This seems like such elementary advice, but as their children enter the years of possible sexual activity, many parents don't really know what their position is on teen sex. You may be against it in general, but what do you feel specifically about your kids engaging in particular acts? When, for instance, do you feel it is appropriate for your child to start kissing? Making out? Touching private parts? Getting naked? What about masturbation? Or oral sex? When do you feel it is appropriate for your child to have intercourse if they are already engaged in a variety of sexual foreplay?

Parents must decide for themselves, taking into account their own religious and spiritual values, as well as cultural mores, what position they will take with their children regarding when sex is appropriate. If you believe sex outside of marriage is wrong or that you should have sex only once you are in a true love relationship, then you need to give that speech and give it as powerfully as you can.

Let your child know that the question of when to have sex is a huge life decision, that there are physical consequences and emotional ramifications, and that each person must ultimately make the decision for him or herself. But, because you love them so dearly, you want them to know your personal position and *why* that is your opinion. This isn't the time to just drop the "no" hammer. It is critical to make your case so they have all the information and input you can give them before they choose for themselves. When you extend to them the respect of explaining it, the chances that they might be influenced by your opinions are greater than if you just respond, "Because I said so," like you might have done when they were 3 years old.

And don't shy away from the important details. Let your kids know that, while they won't get pregnant from oral sex, they can still get STDs like gonorrhea, herpes, and Chlamydia—in their mouths! Talk about sexting and impress upon them that those photos, while perhaps intended for only one special person, can easily get released online, where they will live forever. Explain the possible legal consequences of sending naked photos—some states deem it to be the crime of child pornography, which carries a designation of sex offender. Give the basic parenting lesson about how words (or photos) almost always lead to actions. This isn't the time to shy away or hold back with your children.

■ "Resensitize" Your Children to Sex

Regardless which way you come down on the question of premarital sex, it is very important that you as parents sensitize, or resensitize, your children to what sex really encompasses. This generation has been exposed to way too many examples of raunchy, crude, and objectifying sexual encounters in the popular media. As a result, our kids may very well have a skewed view of what is "normal" or "appropriate." They might think, for instance, that sex should be like the porno clip they saw on the Internet. They need to be taught basic lessons—perhaps the kind of lessons you think they already know—that sex is far more about emotions than it is about a physical performance.

■ The Meaning of "No"

Another important sex lesson you to have to hammer home to your kids, over and over, is the power of "no." Daughters must know that they have the power and the right to always say "no" to anything that makes them feel uncomfortable or disrespected. That "no" should be applied to other girls who are exerting pressure on them to "join the club," so to speak, as well as to boys who are doing everything possible to get the girls to submit.

At the same time, you need to be blunt with your daughters about certain things that girls may say or do or wear that may send young men the message they are interested in sex.

Wait a minute! Am I, a former criminal prosecutor, saying that a victim may be partially responsible for a sexual assault? Absolutely not! No means no. But let's teach our girls to be smart. Wearing a mini skirt without panties and a flimsy halter top without a bra at a party after the football game is going to attract a certain kind of attention. Yes, a woman has the right to wear whatever she wants to wear, but she also should be aware of the impression she is making on others. It's up to you as parents to ensure that your daughters are aware of the way the male brain can work and things that men may interpret as being sexually inviting.

And you certainly aren't out of line if you talk to your daughter about her fear of what she thinks is going to happen to her if she doesn't have sex with a boy—that he will immediately dump her for someone else. Ask her, "Do you really want a boy who goes out with you only because he thinks he is going to have sex? Is that what dating is supposed to be about?" Talk to her about building her confidence and self-worth on something more lasting than a boy who demands that she acquiesce to his sexual desires.

Meanwhile, for those of you with sons, the "no" speech is equally necessary. When they hear "no" from the girl they are dating, they need to show respect (yes, that word again) and back off without hesitation. Sex is not a "conquest." Explain to your sons the great anguish that a girl will go through if she is pressured to have sex before she is ready. And, despite all the assumptions that every boy wants sex immediately, tell your sons that they also have the right to choose when they are ready and to not cave into pressure from their friends.

As a former criminal prosecutor, I must give one more critical warning to parents of boys. Talk to your sons about avoiding situations that could open them up to the dangers of false accusations. Reports of date rape are increasing on college campuses. Many times, the accused boys would come in, shocked that their consensual sexual encounter had turned into a claim of date rape. We used to half-joke in the office that "safe sex" meant that both parties had signed written agreements, stating under oath that they were about to engage in consensual sex. As you can imagine, a false sexual assault report could irreparably damage your son's reputation, among other things. Your sons, as well as your daughters, need to be smart about avoiding sexual situations where they might be vulnerable.

◼ What If Your Child Has Sex?

If you are lucky, you have approached the topic of sex openly enough and regularly enough that your child will feel comfortable telling you when they are about to have sex—even if it is before the time you feel is appropriate. And believe me, this is definitely one of those topics you want to be ready to handle just right. You want to emphasize that while you have firm feelings about when you think sex is appropriate, you are going to be there to support and counsel them in the most loving ways if they make a different choice for themselves.

If they do confide in you, bite your tongue on whatever judgment is spewing forth inside your brain. Verbally knocking your child down with a few choice judgmental statements (or some hysterical screaming) isn't going to stop the sexual activity. Neither is grounding your child or marching over to the house of your child's sexual partner to string them up by the toenails. Trying to punish this behavior rarely works, and more often than not it just backfires by setting up a *Romeo and Juliet* scenario, with you as the evil parents. Any chance of rational discussion goes out the window. In the end, you're just going to decrease the chances that your teenagers will have sex safely.

Take the time now to come up with a plan of what you will say if the situation does arise. Find something that can be delivered in a neutral, nonjudgmental tone that invites further discussion, like, "Well, how was it?"

As painful as this one may be for you, it is a critical time for you to be the best parent you can be. Your child really needs your unconditional love and attention at this time, and you want them to come to you for support. Assuming your children are of legal age (see the following section if they are not), they have just made a very adult choice, whether or not you believe they are emotionally and mentally capable of such a choice. Let's face it; you can't physically control this one, so you must deal with it on a rational, logical level. This is life-changing stuff your child is going through, and you cannot afford to just get angry, stick your head in the sand, or abandon them at such a critical time.

So, have a respectful, adult discussion about *all* the consequences of this action: birth control, STDs, HIV. All of the things that they were told but most likely didn't listen to in their sex education class (and ideally in one of your earlier talks with them) need to be reiterated. But this time, make the talk as specific and graphic and real as possible. To get them thinking about the consequences of sex, for instance, go through the disadvantages of getting pregnant and becoming parents at such a young age. If possible, have someone who had a child as a teenager talk to them about how it changed their life. Get the statistics on unintended pregnancies so they will understand just how quickly it could happen to them.

Make sure they have all the best sex information that's out there—complete and accurate information. Give them good, age-appropriate books written by smart therapists on the consequences of teenage sex. (Leave the books in their room. The kids will read them.)

Also, take your teenagers to the doctor and get a "medical" viewpoint. Have the doctor talk to your child, one on one, about issues of sexuality—from the spread of diseases to the risk of pregnancy and different methods of contraception. Your child might really appreciate an outside expert who will answer their questions. STD and HIV are just letters until your kids see what they look like up close and personal. Photos are always worth a thousand words, right? The only encouragement I needed to use birth control was to see a video of an actual birth. (Unfortunately, I didn't see it until I was about to give birth!)

Finally, this isn't a time to coddle but to inform. Explain the financial cost of buying birth control and additional medical exams. Have them come up with a plan of how to pay for them. You can still express to them your reasons for not wanting them to be sexually active. Be clear that your position hasn't changed. However, as their parent, you want them to be as prepared as possible for the adult consequences they are now taking upon themselves.

■ The Underage Sexually Active Teen

If your child is *not* of legal age, then you have the option of reporting it to the police. If the sexual partner is an adult in a position of trust who has taken advantage of your child's naïveté, I strongly recommend taking legal action to stop a predator. Your child should also get counseling to help them appreciate the significance of what happened.

If the sexual partner is another young person and the sexual relationship was consensual, consider getting together with the other parents to assess the situation. Going through the legal system can be a traumatic experience with lifelong ramifications, for both the boy and the girl. A good kid with a bright future who has a consensual sexual relationship with his girlfriend, who is also a minor, can be branded a sex offender, and his life is changed forever. If the kids are open to listening and cooperating and the facts warrant leniency, you may want to find a better solution, outside of the legal system, that everyone can agree on. Once it goes to court, it is out of your control, and everyone's fate rests in the judge's hands.

If Your Child Is Gay

The same basic rules and principles apply when teaching your children about sex, whether your child is gay or straight. Obviously, you will need to tailor your discussions a bit if your child is gay. But don't let your embarrassment or lack of understanding cause you to just ignore the whole thing altogether. Be open and honest with your child. If you are straight and are unfamiliar with the details of homosexual intercourse or sexual etiquette, explain that to your child. Seek out information and learn together. Reassure your child that you want them to be happy and healthy and safe.

If your child is gay and you are struggling with accepting your child's sexuality, you are not alone. It is common for parents, upon learning that their child is gay, to experience feelings of guilt, anger, sadness, and loss. As you work through those stages, remember that your child is also going through feelings of uncertainty about their relationship with you and whether you still love and accept them for who they are. Your role as parent cannot be put on hold. There really isn't a "pause" button. You have to keep teaching and guiding your child—and that includes dealing with the topic of sex.

12

When to Invade Your Child's Privacy

Should you invade your child's privacy? Ask five random parents this question, and you will probably get five different answers. With my experience, both as a mother and as an officer of the court, I have developed strong opinions on this privacy issue.

As a mother, I'm a firm believer in building a relationship with your children based on trust. It is a crucial foundation for respect and honesty in any relationship, but especially for a child who wants desperately to bond with their parent. Just the phrase "invading my privacy" threatens to undermine the entire foundation of trust. However, as a criminal prosecutor, I know that there are critical times when a parent could greatly benefit from some intimate insight into what their child is feeling, thinking, and doing.

If you are thinking about invading your child's privacy, first evaluate your own motives. Why do you feel the need to dig deeper? Are you a controlling parent, looking for more ammunition to manipulate your child to do what you want him or her to do? Are you looking for more ways to infiltrate yourself further into your child's social circle? Or is your parental gut telling you there is something amiss in your child's life? If your genuine reasons for wanting to snoop aren't centered on a concern that your child is heading down a harmful path, then step back and exercise some restraint.

There are some red flag events that might warrant looking for additional insight into your child's world. Ask yourself these questions:

- Has your child's behavior changed drastically?

- Has your child become completely noncommunicative with you? Are you at the point where you are unsure who your child's friends are, where they're spending their time, and so on?

- Has there been a traumatic event in your child's life that they aren't talking about (such as a divorce, a death, a move, or a romantic break-up)?

- Does your child have a new peer group that makes you nervous?

- Has your child's grades dropped significantly? Is your child misbehaving at school or skipping school?

- Are you worried your child might be using drugs or alcohol?

Taking these questions into consideration, you then need to do a "balancing assessment." Does your concern for your child's well-being outweigh the negative impact your actions may have on the trust in your relationship? Carefully weigh the pros and cons before proceeding.

◼ Making Modern Technology Work for You

It used to be that the only real way for parents to pry into their child's private life was to hunt around their child's room to find their hidden diary, assuming they had one, and then break open the lock and read the private details. They knew that if they got caught reading a child's diary, the relationship was most likely irreparably harmed. There was no way for a child to view such an intrusion as anything less than a tremendous violation of trust. That child would probably never feel secure with his parents again.

And if your child is one who still keeps such a diary and you broke into it, that would still be a violation that could haunt you for years to come. But nowadays, modern social networking gives parents a huge opening into their child's thoughts on a level that our parents could not have imagined. And, as a parent and an officer of the court, I take the firm position that no one has an expectation of privacy in what they choose to put out in the universe. Many kids (and adults) still believe that somehow they can pick and choose who will read their emails, Facebook posts, and tweets. Sorry, Charlie! Once it is out there, it is out there. Anyone who can access it can see it. Photos, gossip, secrets—none of it is private. Your future employers can and probably have seen it. Your boss can see it if you used a work computer. Law enforcement can see it. So, why not parents?

And, interestingly enough, kids today actually want to share very private things about themselves on the Internet— things that they would never dream of telling their parents. I first became aware of this back in the early beginnings of social networking, way before MySpace or Facebook or Google were household words. I was trying to decide whether to file a rape case. The detective submitted the file to me, which contained a sketchy, two-page report of a statement made by a young woman who was claiming that she had been date-raped. There was no physical evidence to corroborate the allegation because she had waited a month to report it. She didn't really have a reason for why she had waited so long to go to the police. The young man she named as her attacker had responded to the detective's request for an interview and had been forthcoming about an on-and-off dating relationship with his accuser. Surprised by the allegation, he said all the sex in their relationship had been consensual and that they had continued to date on and off since the time of the alleged attack. However, by the time the alleged victim made the police report, the relationship had cooled off. When the detectives re-contacted the alleged victim, she admitted that she had continued the dating relationship after the alleged rape.

It was a "he said/she said" scenario, with nothing to corroborate either statement. But the detective had done her job and dug a bit deeper into the backgrounds of both parties. Lo and behold, she had found an online diary written by the alleged victim! I can't even remember what Internet forum was used, but there it was: our victim's life written out in her own words. The detective had printed it out, and sure enough, it covered the time frame of the alleged attack. I skimmed eagerly through

"You're Perfect…" and Other Lies Parents Tell

it—feeling like such a voyeur on one hand but excited to have access to such amazing first-person evidence on the other hand.

And guess what? Although there was not one mention of any sexual assault anywhere, there were plenty of ups and downs about this boy, her alleged attacker, who she thought was her boyfriend but who wouldn't commit to her. Also interspersed through the online diary were the most intimate details about her heartache over losing her mother unexpectedly a few years back.

As a parent, I kept thinking as I read this diary, "Her father needs to know this so he can understand all the hurt and pain his struggling daughter is feeling." It could have helped him to understand her so she wouldn't feel the need to act out in negative ways to get attention.

So, stuff put on the Internet by your child, of their own volition, is fair game. Google your child's name and see what comes up. Check out Facebook and Instagram and Twitter. Look at the photos. Read the messages. You may see your child in a whole new light.

Big cautionary yellow flashing light! *Do not ever* hijack their sites and post things pretending to be your child. I know, it sounds ridiculous. But amazingly, some parents do it. Obviously, those parents are not delving into their children's posts with the right intentions in the first place.

▪ Applying the "Plain View" Doctrine

The other possible source of information that isn't an unconscionable violation of trust is stuff left out by your child in plain sight. In criminal law, this is called the "Plain View Doctrine." Police officers are allowed to look at anything they find in plain sight in a location where they have a legal right to be. If you, as the parent and owner of the home, go into your child's bedroom to clean or put away clothes, or what have you, and you see things that aren't hidden away, if you have a legitimate concern, it may be okay to look.

I did this once when I was picking up some clutter in my son's room. I think he was about 10 years old. I saw a stack of graded homework that had been dropped on the floor. I picked it up and thumbed through it. One drawing caught my eye. I'm guessing the assignment had been to draw your family members. I was fascinated and devastated at my son's representation. He had drawn a typical family—father, mother, himself, three siblings, and then one more female figure, sort of floating up in the right corner. To a casual observer, it would appear that my son had the stereotypical nuclear family, with a strange aunt or something that floated around. However, his drawing actually depicted his father, stepmother, his half-brothers and sister, and himself. Much to my shock, I realized *I* was the floating female, off to the side.

I couldn't believe it! I felt I had been doing the majority of the parental heavy lifting, covering both the father and mother roles as best I could. His father lived nearby and was accessible but not overly involved. I had never heard my son say one word of complaint about not having a picture-perfect family. He and I *were* a family, at least in my eyes. But here was *his* view of it, or, at least, how he wanted others to see it.

And here, my fellow parents, is the biggest question for you to consider if you choose to delve into your child's privacy: What are you going to do with the information once you have it? What if it is painful to you? What if it points to your flaws? What if it reveals things you don't want to know or don't believe?

Ponder these questions carefully, because once you have the information, you can't pretend you don't. And, if you react based on your own ego or emotions or feelings, you may end up causing great damage to your relationship with your child.

I will admit, my first reaction was to hold that drawing up to my son and ask him, "Do you really think so little of me, as I'm trying so hard to raise you right and provide for you, that you make me a little floating figure in the corner? Are we not enough of a family?" My second reaction was worry and concern that my son was unhappy, unfulfilled, and wishing he was growing up in a big family.

So, what did I do? I took a deep breath and put the drawing back in the stack of homework. Then I watched my son carefully for signs of discontent or unhappiness. I suggested and facilitated more contact with his dad. And I talked in general terms about the different forms of families. How did his friends feel about having divorced parents? How did they deal with the split-family stuff? I also listened carefully to what he was saying.

I didn't uncover any earth-shattering secrets. But I did increase my sensitivity to an issue that I had thought wasn't one for my son. Years later, when he was an adult, I found out more about what had been going on in his life at that time. Thank heavens I had not made it all about me. Because it wasn't at all. And increasing my awareness of my son's complex life was probably the best thing that I could have done for him at that time.

Use the Information Wisely

You must commit to not use the information you find to judge, punish, cross-examine, or attack your child. It should be used to *inform your own behavior.* Use it to enlighten your understanding of your child and where they are heading right now. Use it to know where you need to educate and caution your child.

One parent I know did some Internet research and found out that his teenager was starting to go to these parties where the kids would all get drunk and then drive home on some very dangerous roads. Instead of confronting his son with his online boasting and grounding his son, this father started pointing out news stories and photos of fatal accidents caused by drunk drivers. He brought up examples of people whose lives were changed forever when they unintentionally killed someone else while driving drunk. And, this father became much more vigilant about making sure his son wasn't going places where there was no adult supervision. He checked in with his son more when he was away and stayed up to make that physical contact with him when he came home late at night.

Knowing what is really going on in your child's life, especially during their teenage years, can be a huge help in knowing how to parent. But, to paraphrase, with great knowledge comes great responsibility. Take that step carefully. Then use the information wisely.

13

If Your Child Gets Arrested...

What do you do if you get that dreaded phone call? The one where your child's voice sounds scared and helpless as they tell you they are in jail? Do you panic? Get angry? Get sick to your stomach? Wonder what you did wrong? Wonder what the neighbors will think? Do you go into hyper-protective parent mode, rushing down to the police station with both barrels blazing? Do you break down crying?

I guess we don't really know how we will react, unless and until it truly happens to us. But I have had parents call me, desperate to do the right thing to help their child navigate this unfamiliar and frightening process. It is always a heartrending experience to hear these parents so scared about their children's future.

I am going to share with you what I tell these parents. It is based on my 18 years of experience as a criminal prosecutor, down in the trenches, dealing with these situations day in and day out. This advice is also based on being a parent. It is *not* the point of view of a defense attorney. That is important full disclosure, because while it is a prosecutor's duty to "seek justice," it is the defense attorney's duty to provide their client "zealous representation." Most of the time, although not always, a defense attorney does whatever it takes to get the defendant out of as much culpability as possible—regardless of whether the defendant is actually guilty. Most defense attorneys rarely worry about or consider the long-term consequences of "getting their client off." If the client continues to have the problems that put him or her in jail in the first place, well, for the defense attorney, that usually means repeat business.

I don't think "getting off" is the best approach for your child—for now or for their future. The honest, focused, committed parenting approach we have been talking about throughout this entire book applies here as well! The way you handle this situation with your children will speak volumes to them about how they should handle life.

This is a basic outline of the steps to follow. Every case is different. How serious the charges are, how strict the prosecutor's policies are in your area (yes, it is a harsh reality that justice is not consistent), how "by the book" the individual attorney is who gets assigned to your case, how old your child is, how your child has behaved up to this point in their life—all of these things will affect the outcome of your case.

Keep in mind this caveat: If your child is truly innocent, then you should work with their attorney to defend your child to the fullest, including getting the case dismissed and the charges expunged from their record. Sometimes, a truly innocent person is in the wrong place at the wrong time or becomes the undeserving target of an inept, overanxious law enforcement officer (or agency) and gets arrested and caught up in the system. It does happen.

However, the majority of the time, there is a legitimate reason for an arrest. The following tips are for what to do when this happens to your child:

Gather Information

First things first. You need to know what your child is facing. So, start gathering the facts.

What Does Your Child Say Happened?

Caution them that this is the time for full, honest disclosure. Lying or hedging the truth is going to handicap your ability to help them. (Note: A defense attorney would most likely advise you to never ask a defendant if they did it, because the truth can handicap their ability to present their "best defense.")

What Does the Police Report Say Happened?

Every defendant has a right to a copy of the police report. In it you will be able to read what the law enforcement officer is alleging your child did that constitutes a crime. It is only a preliminary report, so there could be more evidence alleged later.

What Are the Actual Charges?

The defendant has the right to know what charges he or she is facing. Many times the code violations are specified in the police report. The law will be named as a specific code (i.e., Penal Code, Health and Safety Code, Vehicle Code, etc.) and section number. The code may be abbreviated.

A Crash Course on Charges and Penalties

Now you need to educate yourself on the specifics of the crime charged and the potential punishment your child is facing. This doesn't take a law degree. Google it first. Find the actual code section. Laws vary state by state, so make sure you are checking the law of the state where your child was arrested. Many of the laws will sound like complicated "legalese," but the language of the code section will tell you the name of the law violated, the elements of the crime, and the possible punishments. The important thing to figure out is how serious the crime and the punishment are.

In broad strokes (and remember, each state has variations, so this is a general guide), there are three categories of crimes: *infractions*, which are the least serious, like traffic tickets, usually just involve paying a fine (no jail time or arrest); *misdemeanors*, which are midlevel crimes that usually don't involve serious injury or violence, are punishable by a possible fine and up to a year in jail; and *felonies*, which are the most serious crimes, are punishable by a possible fine and state prison time.

If Your Child's Case Lands in Juvenile Court

Thank your lucky stars, because in most states, the focus of juvenile court is much more rehabilitative than punitive—almost to a fault. Many times, unless you are dealing with a serious felony, the result is sending the child "home on probation," without much more oversight. It just puts the onus directly on the parent to figure out what went wrong and to fix it before the child ends up back in the same place. If your child gets arrested again, their prior record will come back to be used against them.

Despite less chance of serious custody time (in a youth facility rather than jail or prison), it is still beneficial for you and your child to follow these steps.

When to Get a Private Attorney

This is one of the hardest questions, and there is no set answer. Every criminal defendant has a constitutional right to legal representation. Translation: a public defender. It is always a good idea to have an attorney represent you in criminal court. The question then becomes—public or private?

Your child will be asked whether they want the services of a public defender or whether they want to hire their own attorney. This is your child's choice. Contrary to popular belief, public defenders are not automatically free. Based on a financial assessment made by the Judge, the defendant may or may not be ordered at the end to pay for the legal services received.

Hiring a private attorney will almost always cost money. Even if it is a standard, first-time offense case, like a DUI that is handled in a standardized way across the board regardless of who the defense attorney is, you may end up paying a private attorney thousands of dollars for essentially coming into court and getting the same outcome the public defender would have gotten.

Many people have a misconception that public defenders are somehow not "real" attorneys or aren't the best attorneys. I will tell you from my personal experience that public defenders run the gamut from good to bad, just like private attorneys. There are brilliant public defenders and slacker public defenders, the same as private attorneys. The downside to public defenders is that they usually have a very large caseload, handling multiple cases every day. The likelihood is that the private attorney has fewer cases and more resources and therefore is able to spend more time and energy on each case.

On the flip side, public defenders are usually assigned to the same courthouse, even the same courtroom, for long periods of time. That usually means they know the judge, the prosecutors, and the court staff really well. In many efficient courtrooms, the public defender, prosecutor, and judge build a rapport with each other, forged from hours spent dealing with case after case. A good public defender will know what the best deal is that you can get from the prosecutor who is also assigned to that courtroom and what argument will get the best response from the judge. Many times they will also be familiar with the strengths and weaknesses of the law enforcement agencies involved. This is all valuable familiarity that shouldn't be quickly discounted.

Many times, if a defendant goes with a public defender initially and then, after discussing the case with their public defender, decides that they need a private attorney and makes the request in a timely manner, the judge may allow the change to be made.

■ Make an Honest Evaluation

Before your child starts focusing on what is going to happen, I suggest you help them figure out what path led them to this place. What bad decisions did they make? Are they hanging with the wrong crowd? Are they using poor judgment under the influence of drugs or alcohol?

This is the time to dig. Verbally share your love and concern with your teenager. Explain to them that you want to support them through this process—not to "get them out of it" but to help them figure out what they need to do or change to get them on a different course in life. As a parent, you will have to let go of your concerns about what your friends or family might think, of trying to pin the blame somewhere, of trying to "normalize" the situation. Even if your child is charged with a lesser crime, say a silent prayer of thanks, but still recognize it for what it is—a huge red flag that your child is not going in the right direction. And if you see that red flag, you must take action.

RED FLAG	ACTION
Addiction issues	Time to go to rehab
Psychological or emotional issues	Time to go to a therapist
Learning disability	Time to go to a specialist
Lack of discipline	Time to institute structure

This is also the time to make amends to the victim (or victims) of your child's wrongdoing. (Note: check with your defense attorney first to make sure you do it in a manner that he or she approves of and in a way that doesn't weaken your child's negotiating position.) It is imperative for your child to recognize the impact their bad choices have had on innocent people. Do not just write a check to the victim and say it is taken care of. This is your *child's* debt to pay. Making true amends means more than just money. A sincere apology is not only healing for the receiver but also cleansing for the giver.

One of the best defense attorneys that I ever worked with in Los Angeles was named Charlie English. He was brilliant at having his clients show they were changing their lives and making amends. And he was so effective with prosecutors and judges that I never could understand why more defense attorneys didn't do it. Maybe it was because it took a lot of work or maybe because it required a firm, persuasive hand to get the defendant to agree to it and then follow through. Charlie would show up in court for a pretrial discussion, and before I could even open my mouth, he would hand me reports and letters showing what his client had already done to make the victim whole and to change his or her own behavior. He would do all the groundwork so I would feel like my job was practically done for me. The eagerness exhibited by the defendant to admit his or her mistake and take responsibility, before I or the court could demand it, made us all much more amenable to working out a disposition that would help the defendant stay on a positive path.

◼ Prepare for Court

Document, document, document! In the context of a parent going to court with their child, preparation for court means putting together a file that contains "mitigation" and "explanation." The "mitigation" part should include documentation of your child's accomplishments and good works. Gather up good report cards, achievement awards, letters of recommendation, and service project reports, and organize them in a folder or binder. You can also include documentation that might help explain why your child committed this crime. If your child has any issues that contributed to his criminal actions (i.e., psychological, mental, or physical issues discussed previously), you may want to include a report from any expert who has worked with your child.

Make a copy of the entire file and take it to court with you. (Don't risk losing the originals.) Keep it to a manageable size so it can be skimmed through easily. Your defense attorney can use it to argue that your child has made positive contributions to society, has the capability and desire to be a law-abiding citizen, and deserves a second chance.

◼ Be a Visible Support System, Not an Interfering Protector

Having parents and family members present in court as a visible support system, actively committing to helping the defendant successfully complete the punishment, is a huge asset for a criminal defendant. However, parents who try to exert control over the process, downplay their child's involvement, or perpetuate the child's denial of responsibility can be a liability to their child's case. The court may decide that stricter conditions are required as part of the sentence to ensure that the court's orders are met.

I'll never forget a mother and father I met while I was prosecuting their son, a man in his early 30s. When I first saw the defendant in court, he had the disheveled, unkempt, manic look of a person with a mental disorder. He had committed some serious crimes while in some prolonged psychotic delusions that erupted after he refused to take his prescribed medications. I needed to get him off the streets, but putting him in prison for whatever amount of time without any help for his mental illness was only postponing a ticking time bomb.

Then I saw them—his parents, a quiet little couple with worried eyes. They showed me a photo of a handsome, confident man with a charming smile. That was the defendant when he was in his mid-20s; he was a college graduate, with a beautiful wife and little baby girl, finding great success in his high-powered sales job. Then he started to change, they told me, overtaken by paranoia and delusions. As he spiraled downward, he eventually lost his wife and child, and then he disappeared.

They had traveled from their home, across the country, as soon as they heard that he had been arrested, relieved to finally know where he was. They told me they were committed to doing whatever it was that the court required of them, whatever they could do to help their son. They didn't excuse his behavior, they didn't ask for special treatment, and they didn't try to buy his way out. They worked tirelessly with the attorneys and the court to find a solution that would satisfy the law, protect the victims, and put their son in a safe environment while he got the intervention he needed. The parents' involvement enabled all of the parties to reach a truly just sentence.

■ Respect the System

The criminal justice system should never be taken lightly. When you are dealing with a structure that can take away a human being's freedom, you should never underestimate its power. Teach your children to respect law enforcement and the law before it is too late and they are caught up in it. Don't ever show contempt or talk flippantly about how it is no big deal to confront a police officer.

If you get pulled over for a traffic violation, don't lash out in an angry manner or sass the officer. Because when your child eventually gets pulled over for their first traffic stop and you aren't there to run interference, they are going to be scared and clueless as to how to respond. Very likely, their default response will be to mirror the attitude they saw from you. And let me tell you, dear parents, there is no quicker way to escalate a simple traffic stop into something much more serious than to fail the "attitude test" with a police officer.

Teach your children the proper way to act during a traffic stop. Make eye contact, speak clearly, keep your hands in plain sight, and don't make furtive movements. Reach for documents only after being told to by the officer. A healthy amount of fear for law enforcement authority can go a long way to deterring reckless behavior that can't be undone.

For a short period of my career as a criminal prosecutor, I worked in the same area where I lived with my son. It was during my son's senior year in high school. I told him in no uncertain terms that if he ever did something that got him arrested, he'd better plan on spending the night in jail. I made it very clear to him that he should never expect some type of special treatment because his mother was the head of the prosecutor's office in that courthouse.

I will not say that leaving your child in jail overnight is the right thing to do. I told my son that because I wanted him to respect the system. I also knew, based on his past behavior, that the likelihood he would be arrested and I would have to follow through on my threat was very low. I also knew that the lockup in that particular police station was fairly new, clean, and not too crowded. And I figured I could always sit in the lobby all night and surreptitiously check up on him without his knowledge until it was morning.

It is an individual, parental decision. Jail is not a good place. It is dangerous. It is a place that desensitizes humanity. Most of the time, you as the parent will have no say over whether your child stays in jail. So, do everything you can to keep your child from getting there in the first place.

Getting Expert Help

Not everyone takes naturally to parenting. In fact, most parents are nervous and scared and severely underprepared for the rigors and realities of parenthood. There may be times in your child's life when you see some red flags that cause you concern. Do not hesitate to seek expert help.

Let Go of the Stigma

Some parents are fearful to reach out for help because they don't want to be stigmatized as a "bad parent" or have their child labeled as "out of control." If this is you, let it go! Stop buying into the stigma. That is an outdated and shortsighted view of parenting.

We all know that raising another human being is challenging and complex. No one is automatically awarded all the answers to the daily parenting questions. Getting expert help can be part of responsible parenting.

If your child has a sore throat and a high fever, do you hesitate to take them to a medical doctor to find out what their diagnosis is and get a prescription to cure it? Are you afraid that if your friends or neighbors find out that you took your child to a medical doctor, they will think less of you or your child? Of course not!

Getting help for behavioral or mental issues should be no different. It is clearly no less vital to the health and well-being of your child.

■ You Are Not Alone

One of the things that I do appreciate about the Internet is its ability to bring together people from all over the world who are struggling with the same questions and to provide a forum for ideas and support. You can Google the questions you have and instantly have at your fingertips expert research. You can find parenting blogs and read about other parents going through the same challenges you are facing.

When my son was born 28 years ago, I thought that I was the only new mother on the planet feeling overwhelmed and totally inadequate to the task. It would have been such a relief to hear other moms share their candid experiences. There is great comfort in just knowing you aren't alone. It can take away the fear and doubt and give you confidence to face the issues with action.

■ Red Flags to Get Help

It is always hard for a parent to decide whether their child's acting out is "just a phase" or something more serious. Here are some red flags that you shouldn't readily disregard. There is no set formula for how many symptoms warrant intervention.

In your younger children, ages 3 to 11, watch for the following:

- Hyperactivity
- Severe worry or anxiety that interrupts their ability to sleep or do schoolwork
- Persistent nightmares
- Ongoing disobedience, aggression, or temper tantrums
- Dramatic drop in schoolwork
- Threats to kill or harm oneself

If your child is a preadolescent or adolescent, ages 11 to 18, the potential red flags increase:

- Dramatic drop in schoolwork
- Dramatic changes in sleep or eating habits
- Inability to concentrate or cope with problems
- Acting out sexually
- Depression or severe mood swings
- Debilitating worries or anxieties
- Drug or alcohol abuse
- Extreme eating, dieting
- Distorted body image
- Persistent nightmares
- Frequent outbursts of anger, aggression, defiance to authority
- Strange thoughts, beliefs, or feelings
- Threats to hurt or kill oneself or others
- Threats to run away
- Self-injury

Where to Start

As the parent, you will probably be the first and best person to notice behavioral or emotional red flags in your child. Teachers, coaches, extended family, siblings, religious leaders, doctors, and other parents may also observe questionable behavior. If they share their concern with you, listen with an open mind. You can also proactively seek out their opinions to get a gauge on how accurate your concerns are.

Then talk to your child in a calm, nonthreatening voice. Describe the questionable behaviors to them in an objective, nonjudgmental manner. Ask them why they think they are doing it, what they are thinking at the time they are doing it, how it makes them feel, and if they think it is a nice way to act or an inappropriate way to act.

Sometimes just the discussion can help your child see their behavior more clearly, understand it is wrong, and change. Together you can devise a plan to reinforce the modified behavior. Positive comments from you and other loved ones can help cement the new habits.

But if your child doesn't seem to grasp what you are trying to talk about or refuses to work with you, it is time to seek outside help.

The Experts

So, you are at the point where you think you need some expert help, but you don't know exactly what kind of expert you need. Here are the general definitions of some of the different resources you should consider:

- **Psychiatrist.** A psychiatrist is a medical doctor with at least four additional years of training in psychiatry. They can do medical/psychiatric evaluations for emotional and behavioral issues and psychiatric disorders. They can prescribe medication.

- **Child or adolescent psychiatrist.** This doctor is just like a psychiatrist but with at least two *more* years of training specializing in children, adolescents, and families.

- **Clinical Psychologist.** Psychologists have either a master's degree in psychology or a doctoral degree in clinical, educational, developmental, counseling, or research psychology. They can do psychological evaluations and treatment for emotional and behavioral problems, as well as testing and assessments. They cannot prescribe medication.

- **Social worker.** Most social workers have a master's degree. Licensed clinical social workers can do psychotherapy.

When deciding which expert to consult, do not hesitate to call around and ask questions to determine the best fit for you and your child. There are a lot of therapists out there, with varying approaches and areas of expertise. Therapists aren't a "one size fits all." Find one that seems well versed in your specific issues and who your child will feel comfortable with.

Some other types of experts who may be able to help assess your child are *educational counselors* (who focus on learning disabilities), *art therapists* (who help your child share their thoughts and feelings through artistic expression rather than verbal expression), and *nutritional counselors* (who can evaluate potential nutritional deficiencies that are affecting your child).

The expert will do an evaluation of your child, assessing biological, psychological, and social aspects of your child; putting together a family health and psychiatric history; and requesting blood tests, X-rays, or whatever other special assessments they decide are needed. The expert will then determine a diagnosis and suggest treatment options.

◼ Don't Jump to a Conclusion Too Quickly

Don't panic when the diagnosis comes. Nothing is set in stone. If it doesn't make sense to you or your child, seek out a second opinion. And if you are uncomfortable with the suggested treatment, again, get another opinion.

Many times finding the best solution for your child is a process of trial and error. Sometimes it takes some adjustments to get the medication right or to find the form of behavior modification reinforcement that is effective with your child. Be patient with yourself, your child, and the experts.

And above all, never stop reminding your child that whatever diagnostic term the expert may use, that label does not define your child nor does it change your love for them. Your child will need constant reassurance that all of this hard work is going to bring the entire family closer and will change their own future for the better.

15

Could Your Child Be a Psychopath?

This chapter will not apply to the majority of parents reading this book. However, a few of you may have a child who is manifesting behavior that goes far beyond the bounds of typical childhood angst: expressing violent threats of harm in a calm, detached manner; taking pleasure in inflicting pain; constantly lying, whether they really have a reason to or not, without batting an eye; showing absolutely no remorse or interest when you tell them their behavior is wrong. You may be feeling less than secure, maybe even fearful, in your own home. You may be feeling so apprehensive that when a Columbine massacre or an Aurora movie theater shooting hits the news, you wonder if your child could ever do something so horrific.

Your gut may be telling you that there is something serious going on here, but your heart is in denial that this child could ever really do something dangerous. While this child may seem totally immune to any influence or motivation other than their own strong desires, they may also be charming socially, fun, outgoing, and a confident risk-taker.

This is an extremely touchy subject for parents—understandably so. It is devastating to think that your own child may have psychopathic tendencies. Guilt, fear, and defensiveness may stop a parent from even considering the possibility. Having a better understanding of what psychopathy actually is may help you assess your child's behavior.

■ What Is a Psychopath?

First, let me point out that having the media blithely label every high-profile murderer a "psychopath" has led to many misconceptions about what a psychopath is. I always say not every murderer is a psychopath and not every psychopath is a murderer.

For just a moment, put aside the popular stereotype of all psychopaths being serial murderers, like the movie character Hannibal Lector or Ted Bundy. Too often the images of violent, gruesome murders these examples conjure up are distracting to our understanding of what a psychopath would actually look like to us.

Psychopaths are superficially charming, driven, and arrogant. They don't feel much stress, anxiety, or depression. They are competitive and fearless. Psychopaths are manipulative, dishonest, and undependable, and they may act irresponsibly because they find it fun but then place the blame on someone else. They are lacking empathy, guilt, and love—they may feign it, but they don't really feel it. Without the capacity for empathy or guilt, they rarely learn from their mistakes. Indeed, they don't see them as mistakes.

Reviewing this description, you can see that many of these characteristics may actually help someone to succeed in our competitive world. While not definitive, some experts have suggested that some people with psychopathic tendencies actually rise to prominence in our society—especially in the areas of politics, entertainment, finance, and business.

The studies indicate that about a quarter of prison inmates meet the diagnostic criteria for psychopathy. However, the somewhat limited research also shows that between 1 to 3 percent of the population around us are also psychopaths, functioning as successful, ruthless members of society.

Can Children Even *Be* Psychopaths?

Diagnosing children with psychopathic tendencies is a controversial issue among the experts. Some experts believe that it is inappropriate to try and impossible to do. Many of the adult criteria, such as narcissism and impulsivity, are normal behaviors for children and teenagers. These experts take the position that to diagnose such a conclusion while the child's brain is still developing would be premature.

Other experts resist making such a diagnosis because they don't feel the assessment outweighs the negative cost of branding a child as a psychopath. Let's face it; nowadays if a child is diagnosed as autistic, the response from other parents is sympathetic understanding. On the other hand, if a child is diagnosed as psychopath, I'm pretty sure most of the other parents would be fearful to allow their child around that child.

However, there are researchers who have been studying children with these tendencies for more than a decade now. Some of these experts believe that psychopathy is a distinct neurological condition and that, like autism, it can be identified in children as young as 5 years old, perhaps even 3. And while they still resist the label "psychopath," tending to refer to the children as "callous-unemotional," these experts are optimistic that early detection and intervention could make a huge differ-ence in their lives.

Even Robert D. Hare, the renowned criminal psychologist who developed the Psychopathy Checklist that is widely used to diagnose psychopathy and predict the likelihood of violent behavior in adults, came out with a youth version of the check-list in 2003.

Parents, here is the bottom line: Whether or not the experts put a formal name to it or not, the inescapable truth is that a few of our children are manifesting these behaviors on a consistent basis, and despite your best efforts and all the love you can provide, nothing is changing.

I have a friend who had always wanted to be a mother. She struggled through an abusive marriage for years, got divorced, and finally found a good man and they married. They had a beautiful daughter. My friend was thrilled to finally be a mother, and she relished it. However, as the child grew up, she began to act out in frightening, unfathomable ways. One day her mother caught her torturing the family cat, looking smug at the shrieks of pain the animal was making. Months later, my friend was taken aback as her daughter calmly detailed how she was going to kill her mother by bashing her head in with a rock while she was sleeping. What she found most chilling was the matter-of-fact tone and demeanor her daughter showed, like she was reading the newspaper aloud. My friend dug in, determined to figure out what was going on and what to do to make it better. She did research, consulted experts, and had her child evaluated. No one seemed to know what to do. Her daughter got to the age where my friend felt unsafe in her own home. She struggled with horrible guilt over what to do. Finally, she told her husband that she could no longer handle their daughter and that she had found a facility that would be able to address her needs.

Understandably, her husband was distraught. He told her if she sent their daughter away, he wouldn't be able to forgive her and would end the marriage. What a tragedy for all of them! After trying to hang in there a bit longer, my friend realized she was in an untenable situation. Their daughter was sent away, and the marriage ended.

I have seen the heartache of wonderful, loving parents whose children need help—more than the parents can provide themselves. I want you to know: There *is* hope. Don't give up.

What Is the Cause?

While not definitive, so far the research points to actual anatomical differences in the brain. Magnetic resonance imaging done on the brains of "callous-unemotional" children has revealed a smaller subgenual cortex and reduced brain density—regions of the brain that govern empathy, social values, and moral decision making. Essentially, they don't register negative feedback the way normal brains do. Take away the typical inhibitors of bad behavior, such as worry, shame, and empathy, and you can end up with the mixture of coldness and calculating intelligence found in adult psychopaths. Researchers believe these differences are most likely genetic.

What You Can Do

If you have any concerns about your child, first and foremost, consult an expert. Assessing these traits is a very complex process that should be done only by an experienced mental health expert who specializes in this area of child psychopathy.

Simple behavior modification techniques that focus on immediately rewarding or punishing the behavior may work to decrease some of the anti-social behaviors of a child who appears to be "callous-unemotional."

■ Behavior Modification Techniques

If you are struggling with a child who engages in extreme lying and manipulation, while lacking emotion, empathy, or remorse, here are some strategies that may help you modify your child's behavior:

- Give your child rules with clear consequences.

- When they violate the rule, impose the consequence quickly, firmly, and calmly.

- Don't go into long lectures about their bad behavior. Stay focused on behavior-consequence.

- Use lots of positive talk, praising them when they don't act out in a negative way.

- Give quick rewards for positive behavior, such as "Thank you for not harassing your brother in the car today. You can play outside an extra 30 minutes."

- Spend some time each day giving them positive attention.

- Have them look at you when you are speaking to them.

- If they start to get angry, immediately turn away from them. As soon as they calm down, turn back and give them attention.

It is perfectly understandable for parents of "callous-unemotional" children to want to emotionally distance themselves from their child. Unless you are living in this situation, it is hard to even fathom how difficult it would be to not give up. But the research shows that pulling away from these kids doesn't work. What they need is more positive, controlled interaction with their parents.

However, if you are at the end of your rope, like my friend was, reach out for help. Don't try to struggle through this one on your own or just suffer in silence. Work with an expert. Get a diagnostic evaluation. Find out what you are really dealing with and then get the help that you and your family desperately need.

Parenting Notes

Parenting Notes

Parenting Notes

Part 4

"What Do I Do When...?"

16

Common Questions Parents Ask

What do I do when my child wants to wear something to school that I don't think is appropriate?

In court, many legal arguments require the judge to balance two competing interests in a fair and equitable manner. Here, you have two competing interests—the parenting interest to have your child dress acceptably in public vs. the child's interest, which could be a variety of things, such as to express his or her individuality, reflect a certain financial status, or identify with a specific social group.

So, before you express your initial horror at the unsightly vision that just emerged from your child's bedroom, take a moment to gather some intel. Start with an innocuous comment about the outfit, staying as neutral and nonjudgmental as possible so that they will still be open to responding to your subtle follow-up fact gathering. Is this a new popular style? Your own creation? A way to make a statement? Many times the right outfit is the entrance into a certain clique, and that in and of itself can be hugely illuminating into what is going on in your child's life. Find out what your child is trying to accomplish with the outfit.

Then, do your due diligence on what your school policy is on clothing. Add to that your own policies regarding modesty and age and venue appropriateness.

Now, perform a judicious balancing assessment. How important is the outfit to your child? How legitimate is their motivation? How can you allow them to express their own opinions while staying within your bounds of decency?

Sometimes you can help your child see your point of view without even using any words or lectures. A friend of mine, who is a wonderfully creative parent, had one of her daughters come out dressed for school in a very revealing, overtly sexy blouse. My friend commented that the blouse seemed a bit too much for school. The daughter brushed off her mother's opinion, saying her mom was just too old and out of touch to recognize true fashion, and out the door she went.

The next day, the daughter came home from school and there in the kitchen was her mother, cooking dinner in that exact blouse. The daughter was shocked and embarrassed. She was able to see the blouse in a whole new light, and she never wore it to school again.

How do I get my child to improve his grades?

First, make sure your child has the basics that foster such success—a clean space to work and focus without distraction, a specific time set aside each day for studying, access to resources that the teachers want him to utilize. Turn off the TV, radio, and social media during study time. But be flexible enough to maximize the effectiveness based on the individual child. Some kids like to get their homework done and out of the way the moment they get home. Others need a bit of time to unwind, get a snack, or take a nap, before they are ready to settle down and focus. Is there a problem with attention span? Would shorter study periods with breaks help him keep focused? Know your child.

Then, get familiar with his homework. Where is he struggling? Are there teachers that don't teach and just assign homework? Are there areas where he could benefit from a tutor? (Former students can be excellent, cheap tutors.)

Also, be mindful of overloading your child's schedule. Some kids have so many sports and activities going on that they aren't getting to their homework until late in the evening. Sleep-deprived kids (and adults for that matter) are less effective in learning and retaining information, not to mention the detrimental impact on their health.

I would always tell my son that good grades were a gift to himself and his own future because they would expand his options. His dad, without my knowledge, started paying him a certain amount per grade. The zinger was if he got anything below a C, my son had to pay his dad. I'm not sure which motivator did the trick, but he ended up with good grades.

What do I do when my child wants to do her hair in a style that makes her look odd and extreme?

I always start the hair question with the most important basic truth about hair: Nothing is permanent. It can grow out, be cut, or be dyed. Because of this fundamental truth, I always say err on the side of letting this one go if you can. Kids need outlets to express themselves. Some also need to be able to rebel from their parents. I would prefer the rebellions take place in non-permanent, non-life-altering forms, rather than explode into huge, everlasting manifestations.

When my son was in high school, I came home from work one day to see him looking like a member of the Lion King cast. With the help of a friend's mother (thanks but no thanks!), he had dyed his light brown hair a blotchy black, blond, and red. I was speechless. I took a little comfort in the fact that he said his scalp was burning. I told him that people would judge him and make certain assumptions, whether fair or not, about him as a person based on his hair. But I let him keep it. I decided to draw my line at nonpermanent vs. permanent. He had not gotten a tattoo or piercing, for which I said a silent prayer of thanks.

He kept it for a while and then let it grow out. Later that year, one of his coaches told me that he had always relied on Trevor to be a leader for the team, but that when he dyed his hair, it made him reassess his opinion. I was disappointed that my son's hair color might have had a negative impact on him, but that was a risk he had knowingly chosen, and it was important that he live with the consequence of his action.

How do I get my child to respect my curfew?

Drill into your kids' heads that *nothing* good ever happens after midnight. Danger and violence and crime increase exponentially at night.

If there is is a social pull on your child to stay out with his or her friends, connect with the friends' parents and work together to get all the kids home at an agreed-upon, decent hour.

Set up curfew as a positive way to earn privileges, rather than a constant source of punishment. In other words, rather than acting in response to their violation of the curfew, be proactive. If there is a school dance or a sporting event they want to attend, set up the reward system. If they make curfew for the three weeks leading up to the event, then they can go.

Be consistent in enforcing curfew. I know it is tough to always stay up late waiting for your teenager, but it makes a real statement to your child if they know you will always be there when they get home. Even if you fall asleep, make it a rule that your child wakes you up to let you know they are home. Many times you will be able to get a read on how their night went based on their attitude and body language as they come through the door. You might even be the available listening ear they need at just the right moment.

How do I stop my child from talking back?

There are two keys here—respect and habit. The respect starts with you, the parent. The tone of voice and language you use when talking with your children, your spouse, and others you come in contact with is the tone and language that you can expect your children to use. Watch a family communicate, and you will see similar speaking styles. Practice taking turns talking and listening to your child. If both sides get their time to express themselves, the need to talk back diminishes. Also, when one speaker stays calm and even toned, the other person is more likely to get self-conscious if he is flipping out unnecessarily.

Teaching the habit of respectful communication is critical. I would no sooner sass my mother as I would hit my own hand with a hammer. But I didn't grow up watching and emulating the sassy, mouthy TV characters that fill today's kids' programs. Parents today essentially have to "reteach" their kids proper communication skills. If your kids do spend time watching these very popular shows, you will need to be proactive to counter-act the negative example they are seeing. Don't think that if they start sassing, it will be easy for them to stop. It becomes such a habit, kids aren't even aware of how contentious and rude they may sound. You might try a family experiment where you tell the kids you will be recording the dinnertime conversa-tions or the car rides to and from school. At first everyone will probably try to be on their best behavior. But as time goes on, people will slip back into their normal patterns. Listen to the tapes together and then talk in a nonaccusing way about the patterns you are hearing. Ask your kids how they would feel if someone they admire heard them talking that way.

Responding to sass with the silent treatment can also be a very effective way to show your child that talking back will not bring about the response they desire.

How do I respond if my child threatens to commit suicide?

Never brush it off. At the very least, it is a dramatic cry for help. And it just might be an honest expression of serious intent. Drop whatever it is you are doing. Respond in a calm, support-ive, focused voice. Don't get hysterical or dramatic. Assess the threat to determine the danger level they may be at. Pay atten-tion to the amount of specificity your child uses in his threat. How much thought and planning has gone into this? Have they discussed this idea with others? Are there any possible trig-gering events, disappointments, or traumas that your child has been going through? Are there health issues? Any possible hormonal or chemical imbalances that might make your child more susceptible to this mind-set? Does your child have access to a means to carry out the threat?

If you have guns in the house, get them out or render them inoperable. It is preferable to just get rid of them for the time being. Not having easy access to a deadly weapon forces a suicidal child to take that extra time to think before doing something reckless.

If it is a call for attention, start really listening to your child's concerns. Set up a regular weekly meeting that you both set in stone. It doesn't have to be fancy, just a time that your children can rely on to know they will have your physical presence and your undivided attention to listen to them or to just hang out together. It is amazing how much comfort and sense of security can be derived from such a simple thing.

Educate yourself on what depression is and the potential causes. If you haven't experienced depression yourself or observed it in someone with whom you are very close, you may underestimate the grip it can take on someone's physical and mental health. We live in such an uncertain world now, with horrible life-ending scenarios flashing on every nightly newscast. The doom and gloom are having a powerful impact on our children that we need to remember to consider from their viewpoint. Do not hesitate to seek out professional help on this one, for you and your child.

What do I do if I suspect my child has an eating disorder?

Try to catch it early. Taking a "let's wait and see" approach only allows the dangerous habit to become more entrenched. Find a time and place to talk one-on-one with your child in a loving, concerned manner. Explain what you have seen that leads you to believe there may be an issue. Listen to her response. Body image, diets, and food bombard our kids from the time they can comprehend them. I have heard small children read the calorie information off a cereal box. Adults have unwittingly passed their own weight obsessions to their offspring.

Try to change the tone of your "food" talk to being healthy rather than getting to a certain weight. Explain the long-term detriment that extreme eating can have on her body. Offer to support them (yes, boys also have eating disorders) in incorporating a healthy, fresh food plan along with exercise to do together.

Many times eating disorders are a manifestation of children trying to regain a sense of control over their lives. If that is the case, talk about what real control is and how the disorder actually ends up controlling you. Sometimes, the old-fashioned punishment/reward approach can pull your child out of the disorder if it isn't too far advanced.

I can tell you what worked for me. I left home at the age of 16 to go away to college. I had that high-achieving, perfection mentality that typifies many of the kids who slip into eating disorders. I decided if everyone else was gaining the "freshman ten," I was going to lose ten pounds. I didn't have much money to spend on food anyway, so I mainly ate air-popped popcorn and huge, cheap bags of carrots. At one point the palms of my hands actually turned orange, which the campus health office doctor diagnosed as a result of eating way too many carrots.

I knew I was losing too much weight, but I loved following my rigid, ridiculously inhuman structure, working out too much and eating too little.

When I got to the point of scary skinny, my sister called my parents. Still in denial, I listened as my parents told me over the phone that I was going to go see a counselor about my eating, or else I was coming home. I went to the counselor.

Everything was going in one ear and out the other, until I heard her declare, "...And you may mess up your reproductive system so badly you may not be able to have kids." What? That is what scared me straight. I had already stopped menstruating, so I knew the possibility was real. One thing I knew for sure was that I wanted to be a mom.

There are still times that I struggle with over- and under-eating, but I credit my parents for pulling me back to normalcy. When in doubt, take your child to a doctor. This is an emotional issue that can cause severe physical damage and even death, so don't ignore it.

How do I teach my child to be financially responsible?

Lead by example. Live within your means. I don't believe parents should tell their children how much they make, but I think it is important to share examples of times you are making frugal decisions. Explain that credit cards aren't attached to a magical money tree. Talk about interest rates and the benefits of paying with cash. Teach your child to budget at the same time you start giving them an allowance. Let your children start buying their own "extras" so they understand the value of work and money. Show them that in the real world if they spend the money on one thing, they may have to do without something else. Resist the urge to buy everything for them because it sets up the unrealistic expectation that they should be able to have it all.

When my son was about 8, we were saving every penny for a down payment on a small place that would be just for us. At the time, his favorite car was a Ferrari. One day, we saw a bright red Ferrari in a parking lot. It had a "for sale" sign in the window. My son loved that car! He asked if we could buy the car. I explained to him that we had finally saved enough money for a down payment that we could put toward either the Ferrari or a new place to live. Then I asked him, would he rather live in the Ferrari or in a condo that was all ours? He thought long and hard and concluded that we should invest the money in the condo. That was the end of his infatuation with the Ferrari (but not the Ferrari T-shirt). And he was very happy when we moved into our new place.

And what would I have done if he had picked the car? I would have resisted the urge to tell him "wrong answer" and, instead, asked him questions that gently guided him through the thought process of the practicality of us both living in a Ferrari. It would take some more time, but it would have been practice for him to mentally follow his choice through to its conclusion. Rather than giving him the right answer, he would be learning to get there himself. And he would leave feeling good that he had figured it out for himself.

How do I get my child to follow our religious beliefs?

Ahhhh. There is no easy answer for this one. And if there is ever an issue that demands free agency to choose for oneself, this would be it. However, as long as your children are living under your roof, I believe it is fair to incorporate adherence to the parents' religious tenets as part of the family rules. When the kids are young, it is so much easier. This is the time that your example can make a lasting impression. Religious practices can become part of family traditions. If these are happy memories rather than forced restrictions, there is a higher likelihood that your children will want to continue such patterns in their own homes.

It is usually in the teenage years that the conflicts arise, when kids start caring more about what friends and society think than their own parents and when they are starting to form their own viewpoints. I still believe the best argument to be made to children centers on *respect*—respect for their parents' beliefs, with the understanding that when they become independent adults, they will be free to choose their own belief system and expect the same level of respect from their parents for their choice.

I had a moment with my son about this very issue. One Sunday when he was about 14 years old, I was waiting impatiently at the bottom of the stairs, telling him to hurry up or we would be late for church. He came out of his room, leaned over the banister, and informed me that I should go without him—he didn't want to go anyway. I stopped, taken aback, and looked up at his face. He looked more than irritated. He looked determined. I took a breath, running all of my possible responses through my head, recognizing that this could be a turning point in my son's life. Finally, I just looked at him, and said in a calm voice, "Look, we both know I can't force you to go. You are old enough to make your own decisions. But I'm going to ask you, out of respect for me, if you will please come with me and support me in this because I think it is important."

Then I waited, holding my breath. I'm sure he could see the pleading look in my eyes as he, too, took a moment to weigh his options. Then, without a word, he came down the stairs and got into the car. And that was it. The issue never came up again.

Try to keep the bottom line in perspective—we want our children to be happy, healthy, and kind to others. Realistically, they can be all of these things within many different belief systems. Put your love for your child first and your love for your religion second. And remember, life is long. Kids who try other religions sometimes end up gravitating back to that which is familiar later in life.

One very astute Sunday School teacher who taught teenagers used to take his students to other churches once a month to expose the kids to other religions. They would talk about the similarities and the differences and how the experience made them feel. Once again, respect young people and entrust them with the responsibility of making their own decisions.

How do I protect my child from sexual abuse?

Educate and empower. Use age-appropriate examples of what sexual abuse looks like in all of its various forms. Kids don't know unless someone talks to them about it. Parents and teachers are much more aware now and more likely to talk about it than when I was growing up. If we identify it and label it for our kids, they will understand that not only does it feel wrong, but "Mommy, Daddy, and Teacher all agree that it is wrong, so they will understand if I tell them something happened."

While writing this, I told my mom about an incident that I had never told anyone before. When I was about 6 years old, a young girl and two older boys from our church came over to our house. The boys came into my room and ended up playing naked games with me and the other girl. I still remember the sick feeling I had in my stomach, but I didn't want to upset the "older" kids by refusing. Afterward, I felt guilty and dirty, although I didn't understand why, so I didn't tell anyone. Perhaps if someone had told me before that if anyone ever tried to take my clothes off that it was okay to say "no" or to yell or run, maybe I would have had the confidence to stop it. Or at least tell my parents about the incident afterward. At least I hope so.

Start young, with simple examples. Expand the scenarios as your children get older. Let your children know that if someone makes a suggestive comment about their appearance, they can speak up and say that the comment made them feel uncomfortable. When in doubt, say something to someone. Talk about the forms of abuse that can arise in friend relationships and dating relationships.

Then empower through role-playing. Practice what to say and how to respond in specific instances. Young girls especially are sent the message not offend or rock the boat. The more times and ways you have practiced these situations with your children, the higher the chances of their success in acting without hesitation to stop the abuse immediately.

Should I ever spank my child?

Many of you may be spanking your children, believing it to be a time-tested, accepted parental prerogative. My advice is to stop, and here is why: Violence is a learned behavior. Abused children have a higher probability of becoming abusers as adults. And yet, many parents think that there is a magical defining line between "corporal punishment" and spanking. Unfortunately, there isn't such a thing as a "spank-o-meter" with a dial that lets well-meaning parents know when they are spanking just hard enough to teach a productive lesson but not crossing over to the physical abuse side. Small children especially cannot differentiate between levels of violence. The studies confirm that if parents discipline their children with physical punishment, their children are more likely to use violence to resolve their own conflicts. So, my answer is very clear: no.

How do I get my child to stop texting every moment of her waking life?

Let's face it—we can't just point the finger at our kids. We are all becoming addicted to our cell phones. When we don't have them with us, we feel naked and vulnerable. Our kids just happen to be able to text at lightning speed, while having a conversation and watching television. One of the best things you can do for the health of your familial relationships is put a basket in the middle of your kitchen table. Label it the "phone basket." During meals and family times, *everyone's* phone goes in it—kids and parents alike. Put them on silent so they aren't going off and distracting everyone. Make sure you can see them so no one has theirs hidden in their lap. Kids can text blind, without ever looking at the keyboard. Then, do the same thing at bedtime. Otherwise, your kids will be texting throughout the night with their friends. Curfews don't mean a thing as long as your kids can stay connected to their friends via text. You end up with sleep-deprived children who are doing stupid things over their phones when their judgment is even more impaired than it usually is at that age.

The phone basket is a tough rule for everyone. But it is one of the best things you can do to help your children develop healthy in-person communication skills. Studies are finding that kids (and adults) nowadays are physically addicted to their phones and their in-person relationships are suffering as a result. Help your kids expand their communication skills beyond the keyboard. It will be a great benefit to them throughout their lives.

What do I do if my child plays music that I hate?

Let me tell you, there is no moment in a parent's life that will make you feel older faster than when you hear the words, "Do you call that music?" and you realize that it was you, and not your mother or father, who just uttered them. It is a parent-child battle that is as old as time. Every generation of parents thinks that their children's music is going to destroy civilization as we know it. Satanic messages encoded backwards, misogynist lyrics, filthy swear words. Our parents made the same complaints that their parents made.

This isn't one of the many parental conflicts that is worth going to battle over. If anything, your displeasure will only increase their enjoyment of the offensive music. Part of the thrill for our kids is the fact that we don't get their music—it is theirs, not ours. Music is artistic, creative. Its beauty is in the eye of the beholder. So, try to see the music through your children's eyes.

Ask them what they like about it. Have them play you their favorite songs. Read the lyrics. If they are offensive, ask your child what message they get out of it. Just because your child likes a popular song or continually plays a catchy tune doesn't necessarily mean they are also embracing the offensive message. I've hummed along to some memorable melody and later found out that the lyrics I couldn't understand were embarrassingly graphic.

Of course, it's your house and your rules. And that includes how music is going to be played—what hours, how loud—all of that can be delineated by the parent. Just remember to thank them for their continued adherence to the house rules. And make it a point to expose your kids to all kinds of music. Play classical music, opera, Broadway tunes, the Beatles, symphonies, bluegrass—the list is endless. Make sure to share with your kids your own experiences with the music. What was the theme song at your prom? What was your first concert? Tell them how the music made you feel. That exposure may reshape your child's tastes in music.

My son loved rap music, and when I saw CD covers that had parental warnings on them, we had a sit-down. I asked him what the attraction was and why he was condoning all the swearing of rap, as well as the references to violence against women. He looked at me like I was the clueless one and tried to explain the symbolism of poetry. His face lit up as he talked about the brilliance of these free-styling rap artists who could stream deep conversations to a beat and in rhyme. In fact, he had been writing poetry himself, inspired by the rap music, which he eagerly shared with me.

I saw the music in a whole new light, but I still didn't get it. I said it was okay but insisted that he not buy any more CDs that had parental advisory stickers. My son hesitated and then informed me that there were some CDs that had been sanitized with the swear words bleeped out, but that most of them were available only in their original form. So, if he cut out all the rap that had the swearing and offensive language, it would in essence eliminate rap music altogether.

So, now the ball was back in my court. I truly hated the offensive language in rap and was worried about the messages my son was getting from this music. But I could also tell that he was getting something from the music that went far beyond what I was focused on. It was one of those moments where as a parent you have to step back, take a deep breath, cross your fingers that all of your teachings and values have been internalized by your child, and then let go and trust them. These are some of the hardest moments as a parent and some of the best for your children.

I decided to let my son continue in his love of rap music. But I set down some guidelines. He could play it in his room at a level where I didn't have to hear it. If I heard him start to use those swear words or talk about girls in a disrespectful manner, everything was off the table. And then I kept a close eye on it.

What do I do if my child says school isn't for them?

Listen to their reasons for why they feel that way. School can be extremely frustrating even for kids who want to learn.

Incompetent teachers, subjective grading, mindless memorization, and regurgitation of endless facts can be less than intellectually stimulating.

I am not one who believes that ingesting, memorizing, and then regurgitating data on tests makes kids smart. That's just showing your ability to respond, not to think. But that is how the "game" is played in most classrooms. Many times kids who say they don't like school just haven't caught on to the "game rules." No one likes to suffer through something they don't understand or can't seem to get right.

Sometimes it is a matter of teaching your child how to succeed at taking tests. When I went to law school, I had to learn a whole new way of formulating answers to test questions. Someone had given me a heads-up about how it was almost like learning a different language. So, I didn't take it personally or assume I wasn't mastering the concepts when my first few grades were lower than I was expecting—I just focused more on the format the law professors required, and my grades went up.

For some kids, it could be a learning disability that is holding them back. Your child might benefit greatly from getting evaluated for possible dyslexia or even poor eyesight, which are conditions that can make a child think they are stupid, when it is something totally different that can be corrected or improved.

And then there are the creative geniuses who think out of the box and may truly not need further education. Try to encourage a love of learning, whether it be inventing new things or reading books or exploring the world. There are many ways to find the happiness that comes from stretching your mind.

But be ready to counter the argument "I don't need college" with the statistics on who the jobs go to in our modern world.

There are some jobs that are available only to those with advanced degrees. Many jobs provide a higher pay grade to those with higher degrees. There are also other benefits that come from attending college—the thrill of being around like-minded knowledge seekers, making lifelong connections, the social rites of passage. Just make sure your child has as much information as you can provide them before they make their own decision. And believe me, with today's tuition prices, college should be something your child loves and personally chooses. Otherwise, I say it is the most expensive babysitter you can find.

Should I ever bribe my child?

First, let's clarify what we mean by bribery. Bribery gets its negative connotation from a definition that links promises or rewards with *bad* or *dishonest* behavior. Bribery is a very effective form of behavior modification. Studies on how to form habits—both good and bad—focus on rewarding the desired behavior. I believe that parents can and should use appropriate rewards and praise to encourage good behavior, especially with younger children. This is how we teach them that doing the right thing feels good and brings about positive results. Later, when they have more maturity and intellectual capacity to understand things like character and morality, they will ideally arrive at a place where they want to do the right thing because they know it will bring them internal happiness. But that is character development that we strive for our entire lives.

While our children are growing up, positive reinforcement, from the chart of gold stars on the refrigerator to the healthy treats or more significant rewards, is a powerful parental tool. Balance it with the built-in punishments for the bad behavior. And make sure you don't overuse it so that your child begins to feel like they should be commended for getting out of bed in the morning.

Some parents offer their children a monetary prize if they get through their teenage years without drinking or smoking. Considering the discussion we had on the vulnerability of teenagers' brains to potential addictions, this reward could actually be worth it in the long run. And the desirable carrot may very well help them stay focused when confronted with moments of reckless behavior around them. Then, once you get them safely through the danger years, they can start making more mature, thoughtful choices.

Parenting Notes

Part 5

Letting Go

The Launching Phase

Well, if this was a movie, you would be hearing the music swell, maybe some cellos and French horns, as the two parents stand, arm in arm, in the doorway of their traditional two-story home with white siding, red brick, and black shutters. The camera would pan over the couple, the wife nuzzling her head into her husband's shoulder, tears in her eyes, as he patted her shoulder, whispering stoically, "It's going to be okay. He is a good kid. You did a great job."

The camera would then pan slowly over the beautifully manicured green lawn to the wide, dewy wet residential street. There, walking toward a shiny new SUV packed to the roof, would be a young man, smiling with an excited, happy look on his handsome face. As he opens the driver's door, he turns back to his beaming parents to wave, nod, and tap his heart. Then he ducks into the car and drives off, leaving his suburban childhood behind him as he moves into his perfectly planned adulthood, well prepared and well stocked. And so the parenting years of the cuddling couple come to a cinematic ending. Cue music. Cue sunset.

Well, real life isn't like the movies. There really isn't a single identifiable moment when suddenly your days of parenting are officially over. Sure, there will be those milestones of graduations, weddings, or their first real job with benefits, where you will take a minute to catch your breath, reflect, and mentally pat yourself on the back for getting your child to this point. The phone calls and drop-bys will become less frequent. You may find yourself turning to Facebook or sending off gentle but prodding texts to get updates and reassure yourself your child is still functioning.

And then, gradually, you realize your child is surviving just fine without your constant attention. It is a bit startling when you first recognize that the first, second, and third spots on your continuous worry list don't involve your child. You relax that mental, psychic, emotional grip you have maintained since the moment that tiny being was placed into your arms. And, lo and behold, the earth continues to rotate, the sun continues to come up, and your child continues to breathe and function in the world.

I refer to this as the "Launching Phase," a new chapter in the lives of both the child and the parent. It is a critical ingredient in the recipe for raising productive, independent young adults, and it shouldn't be overlooked when discussing the parenting process. The ultimate parenting satisfaction comes from being able to step back, ideally around that mid-20s mark, and see your child living their own life, balancing autonomy with a strong familial foundation. To get there, you need to pass through the Launching Phase.

Even if your child continues to be enmeshed in more serious struggles, like addiction, you, the parent, must still make your own transition, moving into a different role with respect to your relationship with your adult child. This doesn't mean you abandon them in their time of need. Rather, you help them recognize, whether or not they want to accept it, that they are now an adult—in your eyes and by the standards of society. You cannot and will not coddle them like a little child anymore. You love them enough to let them stand, and falter if need be, as an adult, their own person, with all the privileges and responsibilities that the adult role entails.

■ The Stages of Letting Go

For the parent, this time involves an awakening, tinged with emotions—elation, pride, relief, sadness, regret, and guilt. One way to understand it is to look at it within the framework of the famous "Five Stages of Loss": denial, anger, bargaining, depression, and acceptance. Not everyone goes through every stage, and the length of time spent in each stage varies with each parent. But it's good to be aware of what is happening so you have a better grasp on what you are feeling. And, if you know what is coming ahead, you may be able to better prepare yourself for it.

When I went through this with my own son, I moved through the first three stages pretty quickly. I tend to be practical and task-oriented by nature, so I didn't wallow in *denial*. I'm a big believer in "a time and a season" for many different things throughout life. Parenting is a wonderful, inspiring season, one that actually flows in and out through one's entire life. But it isn't—and shouldn't—be the sole focus of your existence. I am thrilled to be Trevor's mother, now and forever. I am also glad that he has moved on to be a productive, self-sufficient, generous, happy adult. But for him to get there, I had to let go. I did so, knowing that it was what my son needed to be able to move into adulthood. So, get out of their way and let them through!

Nevertheless, some parents get *angry* at the idea of having to let go. Parenting is their identity, their world of control.

They will get mad at their children for taking tentative steps away from the familial hold, especially if the kids are venturing out into arenas not envisioned or approved of by Mom and Dad. If you are that kind of parent, try hard to acknowledge your personal motives behind such behavior. Angry attempts to block this inevitable change will only temporarily slow down the process and could drive a wedge between you and your adult children. It is best for the long-term health of your relationship with your child to get through the *anger* phase as quickly as possible.

The *bargaining* stage can actually be a healthy coping mechanism here because it will require you to think about what you want, weigh it with what your launching child wants, and then work out a compromise together. Communication is always beneficial. Just remember, since we are talking about your child's emerging *adult* life, their position should have equal or greater weight in the compromise. Try to speak up without making demands. It may take some adjustment, but the more mindful you are of your child's new life, interests, and priorities, the easier it will be for them to include you in their new world at a level they are comfortable with, without feeling like they have to keep pushing you away to maintain their new boundaries.

One of the most common *bargaining* issues that parents and children deal with during the Launching Phase is the simple question of how and when to enter each other's homes. Can one just walk in at any time? Should parent and child each have a key to the other's residence that can be used at any time? Should one knock first? Call ahead of time? Permission into your home is symbolic of the new status of both the parent and the child during the Transition Phase. Adult children want and need their privacy from their parents. Likewise, a parent who no longer needs to be available at every second to watch and care for a dependent child may also want to be able to regulate unexpected interruptions.

This issue came up with some friends of mine. Their transitioning daughter happily left the family home to attend college on the other side of the country. More than a semester into her new, independent life, the daughter was astonished to find out that her mother had accepted a new job that was located about ten miles away from her apartment. While the daughter had a warm relationship with her parents, this unexpected close proximity being thrust upon her was not part of her transitioning plan. Worried that her parents might want to slide back into the parenting role with her, the daughter wisely called for a meeting with her parents to discuss the issue. She asked that her parents not drop by without calling first. That way, the daughter had the option to say it wasn't a good time for her, and she could maintain control over her life and her privacy.

Her mother and father prudently put aside any feelings of hurt or disappointment, and they agreed to the requested boundary. In doing so, they were giving tacit acknowledgment to their adult daughter that they accepted and respected her grown-up status.

The parents also decided to ask for the same consideration in return. No dropping by without calling first. This was a smart move for a few reasons—it reenforced the adult child's new perception of her parents as autonomous individuals with their own lives, and it allowed her parents to enjoy their own new level of privacy and intimacy as a couple. It is important for transitioning children to understand that their parents, while still loving them and providing emotional support, may now put more of a priority on their own relationship and other interests.

As for my friends, everyone seems happy with the new ground rules. (There was just one slip-up by the mom, who stopped by her daughter's place unannounced and was firmly reminded of their agreement.) And so far, the Transitioning Phase has been able to continue despite the close proximity.

The *depression* stage was a difficult one for me, as I think it is for many parents of adult children. The root of the depression can come from the refusal of the parent to accept and be happy with their child's new adult status. Or, as in my case, it may come from realizing that suddenly it is over and wishing you could do it all over but better. I feel grateful and fortunate that my son and all my stepchildren have made or are making healthy transitions into the grown-up world. But I wish I had spent more time with my son as he was growing up.

I was a single mother, anxious about the financial burden of raising a child on my own. I also loved my career and wanted to give 110 percent to it. I was lucky to have the help of my mother and sisters in raising my son while I went to law school and worked long hours in the District Attorney's office. But over the years there were too many occasions, when I was caught up in my work, that I sacrificed time that should have been spent with my son. Now, certainly, I could reassure myself and say that this example helped shape my son into the driven, hard-working, self-sufficient adult that he is today. But *time together* is a gift that gives so much more than one can describe in words. The companionship, the ability to speak without limits, the silent affirmation that, "you are important in my life and I like being with you"—all of these messages are best delivered by the act of spending quality time together.

We all make mistakes as parents that may haunt us as the years go by. To be able to get through the depression stage, parents need to be able to let go of these regrets and forgive themselves. One way to deal with them is to share the memory with your child and apologize for it. My mother, now in her 70s, will mention things that happened in my childhood and tell me how bad she feels about it. Most of these things, either I don't remember as being that bad or I don't even remember the incident at all. A lot of the things that she brings up to my siblings and me, we just laugh about now and tell her that is what made us resilient adults. I hope she lets go of her regrets and listens to us when we tell her what an amazing mother she is.

Whatever course of action you choose, whether it is talking to a therapist, apologizing to your child, or writing your regrets down in a journal or letter, find something that helps ease your remorse so you can move through this stage. The truth is, you still have a lot to give to your child.

Acceptance is the stage where you, as the parent, have morphed through your part of the Launching Phase and are ready to stand by your child in your new role. As a parent, you now act as a sounding board—or, to put it another way, verbal comfort food on the other end of the phone. Now that your adult child realizes that, "hey, my parents *do* know some helpful things," you will become fonts of knowledge for everything, from when an injury necessitates a trip to the emergency room to what to write in a sympathy card. It is an exciting new time of life that can be exhilarating and fulfilling for a parent, depending on how mindful and present they are in the first phase of their child's life.

I have a friend who created a beautiful hospice-care company that provides truly compassionate, meaningful end-of-life care that addresses the physical, emotional, and spiritual needs of someone who is about to die. She has seen hundreds of people pass on. She told me that what she has learned is that there are good deaths and bad deaths. For some, their last days are filled with peace and a sense of joy, while others are racked with pain and anger and regret. It all hinges on how they lived their lives and handled their personal relationships. Did they treat their loved ones kindly? Had they forgiven and asked for forgiveness? Had they been honest in their dealings? Had they accomplished the things they had wanted to accomplish? If they had, they were able to accept this wintertime of their life. If not, there was great anxiety and apprehension and denial about the impending end.

I think this happens to parents when they get to the Launching Phase. Did you prepare your children well for their own lives ahead? Did you work hard to be present and not leave things unresolved? Can you now let go and wish them well?

I had a wake-up call to this lesson from my friend, Robert. He was one of the top defense attorneys in Los Angeles and had represented several high-profile celebrities. Robert was well-liked and well-respected by both defense attorneys and prosecutors. He was a tall man, with a lanky stride, a slight stoop to his broad shoulders, and a ready smile as he peered down at you through his glasses. He didn't have to puff or gesticulate like most attorneys to hold your attention. He was always extremely prepared and unfailingly charming. Whether Robert was dealing with a novice D.A., a senile judge, or a demanding client, he treated everyone with dignity.

One year I didn't see Robert around the courthouse for about a month. I found out that his son was running cross-country on his school team and Robert was taking vacation time to travel with him to his track meets. When I heard this, I was actually shocked. It was so out of character for a high-powered L.A. attorney to sacrifice that much time away from work. I also thought to myself, what a lucky young man his son was!

A few years later, sad news spread like wildfire through the courthouse. Robert had passed away over the weekend from complications of a brain tumor. He was only in his late 50s and had just been recognized as one of the top defense attorneys in Los Angeles the year prior.

Robert's death hit me hard. It was the first time someone that I had worked with and felt great admiration for had passed away. In my sadness, I reflected on Robert's life and was comforted by the thought that, from what I had observed, he had lived every day as though it would be his last. He had not lived one way, telling himself that there would be time later to change and start being honest in his dealings, to be kind to everyone he came in contact with, to show his love for his son.

In my mind, as I thought about Robert's legacy, all the amazing trial verdicts and case settlements and public accolades from famous clients blurred together. He had a thriving, successful law practice. He helped many clients, getting them through their criminal cases, and showing sincere interest in helping them better their lives. But I think the most admirable contribution Robert made in his lifetime was the love he showed and the example he set as a father.

We read books and hear experts refer to the "joy" of parenting. As a parent in the throes of this rollercoaster, you may be wondering, "Where *is* that joy everyone keeps talking about? Will there be a day in the future when my very being will be filled with this all-encompassing 'joy' that will propel me into a whole new sphere of 'parental omniscience-ness?'" *No!* That is the movie version, not real life.

What *will* happen in your *real* life is that moments of joy will pop up. And if you actively look for them, they will abound. This is one of the most important keys to being a good parent. *Find* the joy in the experience. Talk about it with your child. Write about it in your journal. Take a picture and put it in a photo album. Celebrate these moments with your children. Let them see and feel the joy you find in your life with them. Teach them to seek out the moments of joy. Appreciate the good. Express your gratitude for it often. It is so true that we see what we are looking for.

My mother frequently uses the two following phrases: "What an adventure!" and "Now *that* was a happening!" Her exuberance for even somewhat mundane things puts a smile on my face and makes it fun to do things with her. And many times, she will say, "We are making a memory." What a great reminder to help us keep every day in perspective! Is this day going to be a good memory that we cherish or a bad memory that causes us to cringe?

I look back over the years with my son and stepchildren and grandchild, and I see so many moments of joy. Indulge me as I give you a short list of my joys that I hope sound familiar to you:

I think of the long nights of rocking my baby and singing him to sleep, feeling that closeness and consuming love for this tiny perfect being. I remember the expression on his tiny face when he would coo with delight. Then I recall watching him march off for his first day of school, so proud of his new backpack. Taking me on a "date" for my birthday when he was 10 years old—dinner at Johnny Rockets and a Wesley Snipes movie. The thoughtfulness he put into the gifts he gave me, including lots of Christmas décor because he knew I loved Christmas! Sharing his heartache with me. Sharing his excitement for the woman he wanted to marry, telling me that she reminded him of me in many ways. Having my stepson always say "yes" when I ask him if he wants me to make him something to eat, because he knows that is how I show love. And telling me how good it tastes. Having my stepsons invite me along for their father-son all-sports weekend getaway. Having my stepdaughter invite us over for a lovely home-cooked meal, including one of my favorite desserts. Getting a spontaneous invitation from a step-daughter to go grab a Diet Coke. Receiving a beautifully writ-ten note of thanks from a stepdaughter, expressing a desire to spend more time together. Watching my new daughter-in-law love and appreciate my son. Going tubing down a snowy Park City hill, everybody strapped together in a big circle, laughing our heads off the whole way. Watching my stepdaughter and stepson-in-law raise the most precocious, loving grandson, who greets me with full-throttle hugs and asks me to read him books. Having spontaneous moments where all the kids are laughing and enjoying each other. Seeing the kids find happiness in their own accomplishments, big or small. Amazing moments of joy to revel in and remember.

It is crucial to document these moments. Save those cards. Take the photos. Don't worry about fancy scrapbooks or lengthy blogs (unless you love doing that). When I first married my husband, I tried to make these elaborate scrapbooks to memorialize our new life together. That lasted about one stressful year. After that, I just threw the photos in one of those albums with the plastic sleeves. Easy and quick—the only organization I did was starting a new album at the beginning of each year. All the kids loved flipping through the pictures, remembering the good times. Then, after a few moves, the albums got tucked away in a cupboard.

During our latest move, I found the albums. I took the time to look through them again. Wow! So much happiness! The kids grew up right before my eyes in the photos. These fun memories had already faded amid our busy lives. Parents, remind yourselves and your kids of your moments of joy.

If you ask the question, "What is the hardest thing you have done in your entire life?" I think anyone who is a parent will give you the same answer: Be a parent. Raising a child brings the greatest joy imaginable and the deepest pain. It is an amazing honor and privilege to be entrusted with the formative years of another human being's life. There is no greater work to be done. Do your best in the limited amount of time you are given. When in doubt, rely on love and respect. And always remember to celebrate the joys together.

Parenting Notes

Parenting Notes

Epilogue

Dear Parents,

I hope this book gave you some insight, some rules to follow, and a large dosage of hope. Please, always remember, positive changes with children don't occur in a particular timetable and along predictable lines. One day goes great, the next day might go just as great, and then on the third day everything seems to be back where you started, or worse: Your kid acts out, and you think everything is a disaster. But the key is to hang in there and keep providing a disciplined but loving and respect-based relationship. And as I've said countless times, respect is the key to teaching values to your children.

Here are some final words of wisdom that I like to call the Serenity Prayer for parents:

> *God, grant me the serenity to accept the mistakes my child must make in order to learn, the courage to hold firm when they face the consequences, and the wisdom to find joy in the process.*

I pray for you as you go through this magnificent journey with your children—and trust me, it is magnificent.

Sincerely,
Loni

"The Partnership Attitude Tracking Study." Drugfree.org/MetLife Foundation, May 2, 2012. http://www.drugfree.org/wp-content/uploads/2012/05/PATS-FULL-Report-FINAL-May-2-PDF-.pdf.

Twenge, Jean M., W. Keith Campbell, and Elise C. Freeman, "Generational Differences in Young Adults' Life Goals, Concern for Others, and Civic Orientation, 1966–2009." *Journal of Personality and Social Psychology*. 102 (2012): 1045–1062.

Twenge, Jean M. *Generation Me: Why Today's Young Americans Are More Confident, Assertive, Entitled, and More Miserable Than Ever Before*. New York: Free Press, 2006.

"Tyler Clementi." *The New York Times*. March 16, 2012. http://topics.nytimes.com/top/reference/timestopics/people/c/tyler_clementi/index.html.

Chapter 2

"Aggressive 'Helicopter' Parents Force Egg Hunt Cancellation." *USA Today*, March 26, 2012. http://usatoday30.usatoday.com/news/nation/story/2012-03-26/easter-egg-hunt-parents/53779670/1.

The American Psychological Association. "Stress in America Findings." November 9, 2010. www.apa.org/news/press/releases/stress/national-report.pdf.

Begley, S. "How Stressed Parents Scar Their Kids." *The Daily Beast*, September 12, 2011. www.thedailybeast.com/articles/2011/09/12/parents-depression-and-stress-leaves-lasting-mark-on-children-s-dna.html.

Brown, Stuart and Christopher Vaughn. *Play: How it Shapes the Brain, Opens the Imagination, and Invigorates the Soul*. New York: Penguin Group, 2010.

Caulfield, Philip. "Laptop Shooting Dad Would Do It Again." *New York Daily News*, February 13, 2012. http://articles.nydailynews.com/2012-02-13/news/31056855_1_facebook-posts-laptop-tommy-jordan.

Celizic, Mike. "Mom lets 9-year-old take subway home alone." NBCNews.com, April 3, http://today.msnbc.msn.com/id/23935873/ns/today-today_news/t/mom-lets-9-year-old-take-subway-home-alone/.

CommuniKids. "Mandarin, French, and Spanish Language Immersion Summer Camp." www.communikids.com/our-programs-/summer-programs.

Corrigan, Maureen. "Tiger Mothers: Raising Children the Chinese Way." NPR.org, January 11, 2011. www.npr.org/2011/01/11/132833376/tiger-mothers-raising-children-the-chinese-way.

Dailey, Kate. "Report Shows Teen Girls Are Drinking More Than Boys, for Different Reasons." *The Daily Beast*, June 28, 2010. www.thedailybeast.com/newsweek/2010/06/29/study-shows-teen-girls-are-drinking-more-for-different-reasons-than-boys.html.

DisneyFamily.com. "Is Your Kid Overscheduled?" http://family.go.com/parenting/pkg-back-to-school/article-747597-overscheduled-kids-t/.

Essex, Marilyn J., W. Thomas Boyce, Clyde Hertzman, Lucia L. Lam, Jeffrey M. Armstrong, Sarah M. A. Neumann, Michael S. Kobor. "Epigenetic Vestiges of Early Developmental Adversity: Childhood Stress Exposure and DNA Methylation in Adolescence." *Child Development*. September 1, 2011. doi: 10.1111/j.1467-8624.2011.01641.x.

"Excessive Stress Disrupts the Architecture of the Developing Brain: Working Paper No. 3." National Scientific Council on the Developing Child, 2005. www.developingchild.harvard.edu.

Gardner, Phil. "Parent Involvement in the College Recruiting Process: To What Extent?" CERI, 2007. http://ceri.msu.edu/publications/pdf/ceri2-07.pdf.

Gibbs, Nancy. "The Growing Backlash Against Overparenting." *Time Magazine*, November 30, 2009. www.time.com/time/magazine/article/0,9171,1940697-2,00.html.

Gottman, John. *Why Marriages Succeed or Fail: And How You Can Make Yours Last*. New York: Simon & Schuster, 1995.

References

Introduction
Twenge, J.M., & Campbell, W.K., *The Narcissism Epidemic: Living in the Age of Entitlement*, New York: Free Press, 2009.

Chapter 1
"A Thin Line: 2009 AP-MTV Digital Abuse Study." http://www.athinline.org/MTV-AP_Digital_Abuse_Study_Executive_Summary.pdf.

Alsop, Ron. "The 'Trophy Kids' Go to Work." *The Wall Street Journal*, October 21, 2008. http://online.wsj.com/article/SB122455219391652725.html.

American Cancer Society. "Child and Teen Tobacco Use." November 8, 2012. http://www.cancer.org/cancer/cancercauses/tobaccocancer/childandteentobaccouse/child-and-teen-tobacco-use-child-and-teen-tobacco-use.

Annals of Psychotherapy & Integrative Health. "College Students Have Less Empathy Than in Past, Study Shows." June 4, 2010. www.annalsofpsychotherapy.com/articles/news/149/15/College-Students-Have-Less-Empathy-Than-in-Past-Study-Shows.

Aspen Education Group. "Narcissistic and Entitled to Everything! Does Gen Y Have Too Much Self-Esteem?" www.aspeneducation.com/article-entitlement.html.

Baldwin, Bruce A. *Beyond the Cornucopia Kids*. Wilmington, N.C: Direction Dynamics, 1988.

Centers for Disease Control and Prevention. "HIV Among Youth." December 2, 2011. www.cdc.gov/hiv/youth/index.htm.

Centers for Disease Control and Prevention. "Youth Risk Behavior Surveillance System: US." *Morbidity and Mortality Weekly Report*. 59(SS-5); 2010 June.

"Children would rather become popstars than teachers or lawyers." *The Telegraph*, October 1, 2009. www.telegraph.co.uk/education/educationnews/6250626/Children-would-rather-become-popstars-than-teachers-or-lawyers.html.

"College students think they're so special." NBCNews.com, February 27, 2007. www.msnbc.msn.com/id/17349066/ns/health-mental_health/t/college-students-think-theyre-so-special/#.UGvW4I64LHg.

Josephson Institute Center for Youth Ethics. "The Ethics of American Youth: 2000 Report Card." Accessed May 1, 2012. http://charactercounts.org/programs/reportcard/2000/index.html.

Josephson Institute Center for Youth Ethics. "The Ethics of American Youth: 2008 Report Card." Accessed May 1, 2012. http://charactercounts.org/programs/reportcard/2008/index.html.

Josephson Institute Center for Youth Ethics. "The Ethics of American Youth: 2010 Report Card." October 26, 2010. http://charactercounts.org/programs/reportcard/2010/installment01_report-card_bullying-youth-violence.html.

Karimi, Faith. "Middle schoolers bully bus monitor, 68, with stream of profanity, jeers," CNN.com, June 23, 2012. www.cnn.com/2012/06/21/us/new-york-bullied-bus-monitor/index.html.

Kennedy, Helen. "Phoebe Prince, South Hadley High School's 'new girl,' driven to suicide by teenage cyber bullies." *NY Daily News*, March 29, 2010, accessed June 23, 2012. http://articles.nydailynews.com/2010-03-29/news/27060348_1_facebook-town-hall-meetings-school-library.

Miller, Joshua Rhett. "Police: Bullied bus monitor won't seek criminal charges against students." FoxNews.com, June 21, 2012, accessed June 22, 2012. www.foxnews.com/us/2012/06/21/bullied-bus-monitor-receives-more-than-120g-in-online-donations/.

National Institute on Drug Abuse. *Monitoring the Future National Results on Adolescent Drug Use: Overview of Key Findings, 2009*. By Lloyd Johnston, Patrick O'Malley, Jerald Bachman, and John Schulenberg. NIH Publication No. 10-7583. May 2010. http://monitoringthefuture.org/pubs/monographs/overview2009.pdf.

Moffitt, Terrie, Louise Arseneault, Daniel Belsky, Nigel Dickson, Robert Hancox, HonaLee Harrington, Renate Houts, Richie Poulton, Brent Roberts, Stephen Ross, Malcolm Sears, W. Murray Thomson, and Avshalom Caspi. "A Gradient of Childhood Self-Control Predicts Health, Wealth, and Public Safety." *Proceedings of the National Academy of Sciences*, 108, (2010): 2693-2698. www.pnas.org/content/108/7/2693.full.

National Institute on Alcohol Abuse and Alcoholism. *Underage Drinking*. March 2012. http://pubs.niaaa.nih.gov/publications/UnderageDrinking/Underage_Fact.pdf.

Rowling, JK interviewed by Oprah Winfrey. "The Long Road to Success," 1:31, September 29, 2010, www.oprah.com/oprahshow/The-Long-Road-to-Success-Video.

Young, Steve. *Great Failures of the Extremely Successful: Mistakes, Adversity, Failure and Other Stepping Stones to Success*. Beverly Hills, CA: Tallfellow Press, 2002.

Chapter 5

Grant, BF. "Estimates of US Children Exposed to Alcohol Abuse and Dependence in the Family." *American Journal of Public Health*. 90 (2000), 112–114.

Johnston, Lloyd, Patrick O'Malley, Jerald Bachman, and John Schulenberg. "Monitoring the Future National Survey Results on Drug Use, 1975–2011: Volume I, Secondary School Students." The University of Michigan Institute for Social Research, 2011. www.monitoringthefuture.org/pubs/monographs/mtf-vol1_2011.pdf.

Substance Abuse and Mental Health Services Administration. *Results from the 2009 National Survey on Drug Use and Health: Volume I. Summary of National Findings (Office of Applied Studies, NSDUH Series H-38A, HHS Publication No. SMA 10-4586 Findings)*. Rockville, MD: 2010.

Substance Abuse and Mental Health Services Administration, Center for Behavioral Health Statistics and Quality. *The DAWN Report: Highlights of the 2010 Drug Abuse Warning Network (DAWN) Findings on Drug-Related Emergency Department Visits*. Rockville, MD: 2010. www.samhsa.gov/data/2k12/DAWN096/ SR096EDHighlights2010.pdf.

Chapter 8

Hsu, Christine. "Families Who Eat at the Dinner Table are the Healthiest." *Medical Daily*, April 24, 2012. www.medicaldaily.com/articles/9661/20120424/family-children-meal-food-communal-dinner-table.htm.

The National Center on Addiction and Substance Abuse at Columbia University. "The Importance of Family Dinners IV." September, 2007. http://www.casacolumbia.org/ download.aspx?path=/UploadedFiles/30dqhuyg.pdf.

Chapter 9

The Corporate Social Responsibility Newswire. "Survey: Parents Let Their Own Experiences Affect Drug and Alcohol Boundaries Set for Teens at Prom and Graduation Parties." May 29, 2008. www.csrwire.com/press_releases/16519-Survey-Parents-Let-Their-Own-Experiences-Affect-Drug-and-Alcohol-Boundaries-Set-for-Teens-at-Prom-and-Graduation-Parties-#.

Enoch, Mary-Anne, and David Goldman. "The genetics of alcoholism and alcohol abuse." *Current Psychiatry Reports*. 2001 Apr; 3(2): 144-51.

Genetic Science Learning Center. "Environmental Risk Factors for Addiction." Learn. Genetics, August 6, 2012. http://learn.genetics.utah.edu/content/addiction/factors/ environment.html.

Genetic Science Learning Center. "Timing and Circumstances Influence Addiction." Learn.Genetics, October 5, 2012. http://learn.genetics.utah.edu/content/addiction/ factors/.

Haiman, Peter. "What Every Parent Needs to Know." www.peterhaiman.com/articles/
whatEveryParentNeeds.shtml.

Johns Hopkins. "Young Students Programs." http://cty.jhu.edu/summer/grades2-6/.

"Judge William Adams Won't Be Charged Over Videotaped Beating Of Daughter,
Police Say." *The Huffington Post*, November 4, 2011. www.huffingtonpost.
com/2011/11/03/judge-william-adams-video-beating-daughter_n_1075284.html.

Kim, Ann. "Two Sentenced in Elaborate Scheme to Cheat on Law School Entry Test."
Los Angeles Times, January 27, 2000. http://articles.latimes.com/2000/jan/27/local/
me-58227.

Ludden, Jennifer. "Helicopter Parents Hover in the Workplace." NPR.org, February 6,
2012. http://m.npr.org/story/146464665.

Markham, Laura. "What's Wrong with Permissive Parenting?" www.ahaparenting.com/
parenting-tools/positive-discipline/permissive-parenting.

Milbank, Dana. "Welcome to Camp Competitive." *The Washington Post*, June 1, 2012.
www.washingtonpost.com/opinions/welcome-to-camp-competitive/2012/06/01/
gJQA0ZgP7U_story.html.

Mind Tools. "The Holmes and Rahe Stress Scale: Understanding the Impact of Long-term
Stress." www.mindtools.com/pages/article/newTCS_82.htm.

Partnership for a Drug-Free America and MetLife Foundation. "2009 Partnership Attitude
Tracking Study." www.drugfree.org/newsroom/full-report-and-key-findings-the-
2009-partnership-attitude-tracking-study-sponsored-by-metlife-foundation.

Paton, Graeme. "Competitive Parents 'Taking Joy Out of Childhood.'" *The Telegraph*,
January 27, 2012. www.telegraph.co.uk/education/educationnews/9044234/
Competitive-parents-taking-joy-out-of-childhood.html.

Paul, Margaret. "The Permissive Parent." December 31, 2006. www.innerbonding.com/
show-article/184/the-permissive-parent.html.

Quiver Farm. "Chick Hatching Project Instruction Manual." www.quiverfarm.com/
Documents/chick_hatching_ project_instruction_manual.pdf.

Rettner, Rachael. "'Helicopter' Parents Have Neurotic Kids, Study Suggests." LiveScience,
June 3, 2010. www.livescience.com/10663-helicopter-parents-neurotic-kids-study-
suggests.html.

TutorWhiz. "Elementary School Tutoring." http://tutorwhiz.schools.com/grade/
elementary-school-tutoring.html.

U.S. Department of Health and Human Services, Centers for Disease Control and
Prevention. *The Effects of Childhood Stress on Health Across the Lifespan*. By Jennifer
Middlebrooks and Natalie Audage. 2008. www.cdc.gov/ncipc/pub-res/pdf/
childhood_stress.pdf.

Chapter 3

"Heroes Among Us." *People Magazine*. www.people.com/people/archive/topic/
0,,20202692,00.html.

Chapter 4

The Colonel's Kitchen. "5 Lessons-The Colonel's Way of Doing Business..." http://
kfc.forumup.co.uk/about178-0.html.

ContactMusic.com. "Spielberg Recalls University Rejection." September 29, 2004.
www.contactmusic.com/news-article/spielberg-recalls-university-rejection.

Dahl, Roald. *Willy Wonka and the Chocolate Factory*. New York: Alfred A. Knopf, 1964.

Lehrer, Jonah. "Don't! The Secret of Self-Control." *The New Yorker*, May 18, 2009.
www.newyorker.com/reporting/2009/05/18/090518fa_fact_lehrer.

Matthews, Gail. "Written Goal Study." Dominican University. http://cdn.sidsavara.com/
wp-content/uploads/2008/09/researchsummary2.pdf.

Giedd, Jay N, Jonathan Blumenthal, Neal O. Jeffries, F. X. Castellanos, Hong Liu, Alex Zijdenbos, Tomas Paus, Alan C. Evans, and Judith Rapoport. "Brain development during childhood and adolescence: a longitudinal MRI study." *Nature Neuroscience*, 2 (1999): 861-3.

Giedd, Jay N. "Structural magnetic resonance imaging of the adolescent brain." *Annals of the New York Academy of Sciences*. 1021 (2004): 77–85.

Hingson, Ralph, Timothy Heeren, and Michael R. Winter. "Age at drinking onset and alcohol dependence: Age at onset, duration, and severity." *Archives of Pediatrics and Adolescent Medicine*. 160 (2006): 739–746. PMID: 16818840.

Hoffman, Matthew. "Prescription Drug Abuse: Who Gets Addicted and Why?" WebMD, October 30, 2008. www.webmd.com/pain-management/features/prescription-drug-abuse-who-gets-addicted-and-why.

Melemis, Steven. "The Genetics of Addiction." Addictions and Recovery.com, March 26, 2012. www.addictionsandrecovery.org/is-addiction-a-disease.htm.

"Millions Of Young People Have Used Cough Syrup To Get High." *Science Daily*, January 13, 2008. www.sciencedaily.com/releases/2008/01/080112181400.htm.

The National Center on Addiction and Substance Abuse at Columbia University. "Adolescent Substance Use: America's #1 Health Problem." June, 2011. www.casacolumbia.org/upload/2011/20110629adolescentsubstanceuse.pdf.

National Institute on Drug Abuse. "What are the early signs of risk that may predict later drug abuse?" October, 2003. www.drugabuse.gov/publications/preventing-drug-abuse-among-children-adolescents/chapter-1-risk-factors-protective-factors/what-are-early-signs-.

National University of Ireland, Gatway. "Health Promotion Messages: To Scare or Not to Scare?" October, 2003. www.nuigalway.ie/health_promotion/documents/J_Sixsmith/2003_scare_ tactics_policy.pdf.

Perrone, Matthew. "After 'Bath Salts' Ban, Legal Ways to get High Remain." Today.com, July 25, 2012. www.today.com/id/48317804/ns/today-today_health/t/after-bath-salts-ban-legal-ways-get-high-remain/#.UPnG0B08DTp.

Prescott, Carol Ann and Kenneth S. Kendler. "Genetic and environmental contributions to alcohol abuse and dependence in a population-based sample of male twins." *American Journal of Psychiatry*. 156(1999): 34-40.

Simons-Morton, Bruce, and Tilda Farhat. "Recent Findings on Peer Group Influences on Adolescent Substance Use." *The Journal of Primary Prevention*. 31(2010): 191-208. www.ncbi.nlm.nih.gov/pmc/articles/PMC3313483/.

"Teenagers using nutmeg to get high." KABC-TV.com, December 3, 2010. http://abclocal.go.com/kabc/story?section=news/health&id=7821597.

Trudeau, Michelle. "More Students Turning Illegally to 'Smart' Drugs." NPR.org, February 5, 2009. www.npr.org/templates/story/story.php?storyId=100254163.

U.S. Department of Health and Human Services. "Maturation of the Pre-frontal Cortex." www.hhs.gov/opa/familylife/tech_assistance/etraining/adolescent_brain/Development/prefrontal_cortex/.

"Vodka Tampons? Reported Alcohol Abuse Among Teens Also Includes 'Butt Chugging.'" *The Huffington Post Canada*, November 14, 2011. www.huffingtonpost.ca/2011/11/14/vodka-tampon-teens_n_1092594.html.

Walsh, David. *Why do they act that way? A survival guide to the adolescent brain for you and your teen*. New York: Free Press, 2004.

Chapter 10

A Day Without Media. Phillip Merrill College of Journalism. http://withoutmedia.wordpress.com/.

ACT Raising Safe Kids. "Media Violence and Aggression: Recent Studies Link Exposure to Violence in the Media and Subsequent Aggression in Teenagers Act for Strong Families." http://actagainstviolence.apa.org/specialtopics/mediaviolence.html.

The American Academy of Family Physicians. "Violence, Media (Position Paper)." 2004. www.aafp.org/online/en/home/policy/policies/v/violencemedia.html.

American Academy of Pediatrics. *Media Violence*. Committee on Public Education. *Pediatrics*, 108 (2001): 1222-6.

American Psychological Association. "Violence on Television: What do Children Learn? What Can Parents Do?" 1999. www.cmu.edu/CSR/case_studies/tv_violence.html.

Beresin, Eugene. "The Impact of Media Violence on Children and Adolescents: Opportunities for Clinical Interventions." www.aacap.org/cs/root/developmentor/the_impact_of_media_violence_on_children_and_adolescents_opportunities_for_clinical_interventions.

Boyse, Kyla. "Television and Children." University of Michigan Health System, August, 2010. www.med.umich.edu/yourchild/topics/tv.htm.

Braxton, Greg. "TV Violence Poses Risk to Viewers, Study Says." *LA Times*, February 7, 1996. http:// articles.latimes.com/1996-02-07/entertainment/ca-33097_1_tv-violence.

Bryant, J. "Frequency of Exposure, Age of Initial Exposure and Reactions to Initial Exposure to Pornography." Presented to the Attorney General's Commission on Pornography. March, 1985. Houston, Texas.

Bryant, J., & Brown D. "Uses of Pornography." In *Pornography: Research Advances & Policy Considerations* edited by D. Zillman and J Bryant. New Jersey: L. Erlbaum & Assoc, 1989.

Changing the Channels. "Major Studies on Television Violence." 2006. http://changingchannels.org/pages/articles/effects-of-tv/major-studies.php.

Congressional Public Health Summit. "Joint Statement of Entertainment Violence on Children." July 26, 2000. http://www2.aap.org/advocacy/releases/jstmtevc.htm.

"Cyber-Bullying: What Parents Can Do About It." Center for Parenting Education. http://centerforparentingeducation.org/library-of-articles/handling-bullying-issues/cyber-bullying-what-parents-can-do-about-it/.

DeAngelis, Tori. "Web Pornography's Effect on Children." November, 2007. www.apa.org/monitor/nov07/webporn.aspx.

Federal Bureau of Investigation. "A Parent's Guide to Internet Safety." www.fbi.gov/stats-services/publications/parent-guide/parent-guide.

Fisher, Deborah, Douglas L. Hill, Joel W. Grube, Melina M. Bersamin, Samantha Walker, and Enid L. Gruber. "Televised Sexual Content and Parental Mediation: Influences on Adolescent Sexuality." *Media Psychology*. 12(2009): 121-147. www.ncbi.nlm.nih.gov/pmc/articles/PMC3086268/#R63.

"GENERATION M2: Media in the Lives of 8- to 18-year-olds." A Kaiser Family Foundation Study, 2010. www.kff.org/entmedia/upload/mh012010presentL.pdf.

Healy, Jane. "Understanding TV's Effects on the Developing Brain." AAP News. May 1998.

Johnson, Jeffrey G., Patricia Cohen, Elizabeth M. Smailes, Stephanie Kasen, and Judith S. Brook. "Television Viewing and Aggressive Behavior During Adolescence and Adulthood." *Science*. 295 (2002):, 2468-2471.

Kubey, Robert, and Mihaly Csikszentmihalyi. "Television Addiction Is No Mere Metaphor." *Scientific American*, January 1, 2004. www.scientificamerican.com/article.cfm?id=television-addiction-is-n.

Louge, Nathalie. "Adolescents and the Internet." October, 2006. www.actforyouth.net/resources/rf/rf_internet_1006.pdf.

Meikle, James. "Twitter Is Harder to Resist Than Cigarettes and Alcohol, Study Finds." *The Guardian*, February 3, 2012. www.guardian.co.uk/technology/2012/feb/03/twitter-resist-cigarettes-alcohol-study.

Papadopoulos, Linda. "Sexualization of Young People: Review." www.drlinda.co.uk/pdfs/sexualisation_review.pdf.

Parents Television Council. "Facts and TV Statistics." www.parentstv.org/ptc/facts/mediafacts.asp.

Parents Television Council. "Sexualized Teen Girls: Tinseltown's New Target. A Study of Teen Female Sexualization in Prime-Time TV." December, 2010. www.parentstv.org/FemaleSexualization/Study/Sexualized_Teen_Girls.pdf.

Senate Committee on the Judiciary. "Children, Violence, and the Media: A Report for Parents and Policy Makers." September 14, 1999.

Strasburger, Victor C. "Children, Adolescents, and the Media." *Current Problems in Pediatric and Adolescent Health Care.* 34 (2004): 49–120.

Surgeon General's Scientific Advisory Committee on Television and Social Behavior. *Television and Growing Up: The Impact of Televised Violence.* Washington, DC: U.S. Government Printing Office, 1972.

"Talking With Kids About Tough Issues." *A Kaiser Family Foundation Study.* February 19, 1997. www.kff.org/youthhivstds/1230-talkings.cfm.

"Teens and Sex: The Role of Popular TV." *A Kaiser Family Foundation Study.* July, 2001. www.kff.org/entmedia/upload/Teens-Sex-The-Role-of-Popular-Television-Fact-Sheet-May-2000-Fact-Sheet.pdf.

Wolak, Janis, Kimberly Mitchell, and David Finkelhor. "Unwanted and Wanted Exposure to Online Pornography in a National Sample of Youth Internet Users." *Pediatrics.* 119 (2007): 247-257. doi: 10.1542/peds.2006-1891.

Chapter 11

Gardner, Amanda. "More Than Forty Percent of U.S. Teens Have Had Sex," *U.S. News,* June 2, 2010. http://health.usnews.com/health-news/family-health/womens-health/articles/2010/06/02/more-than-40-of-us-teens-have-had-sex.

Jayson, Sharon. "Sex Study: More Teens, Young Adults Are Virgins." USATODAY.com, March 3, 2011. http://abstainpureandsimple.org/SexStudyMoreTeensYoungAdultsareVirgins.htm.

Pittman, Genevra. "'Sexting' Linked to Risky Sex Among Teens," Today.com, September 17, 2012. http://todayhealth.today.com/_news/2012/09/17/13918225-sexting-linked-to-risky-sex-among-teens?lite.

Quenqua, Douglas. "Sex Life of Teenagers Is Subject of Study," *The New York Times,* August 16, 2012. www.nytimes.com/2012/08/16/health/data-suggest-teenagers-not-more-likely-to-have-oral-sex-first.html?_r=0.

Rice, Eric, Harmony Rhoades, Hailey Winetrobe, Monica Sanchez, Jorge Montoya, Aaron Plant, and Timothy Kordic. "Sexually Explicit Cell Phone Messaging Associated With Sexual Risk Among Adolescents." *Pediatrics.* Published online September 17, 2012. doi: 10.1542/peds.2012-0021. http://pediatrics.aappublications.org/content/early/2012/09/12/peds.2012-0021.abstract.

Sheehy, Kelsey. "Tips for Parents to Address Teen Sexting." USA News: Education. July 18, 2012. www.usnews.com/education/blogs/high-school-notes/2012/07/18/tips-for-parents-to-address-teen-sexting.

Temple, Jeff R., Jonathan A. Paul, Patricia van den Berg, Vi Donna Le, Amy McElhany, Brian W. Temple. "Teen Sexting and Its Association With Sexual Behaviors." *Archives of Pediatric and Adolescent Medicine.* 166(2012): 828-833. http://archpedi.jamanetwork.com/article.aspx?articleid=1212181.

Weintraub, Karen. "More Teens Have Oral Sex Earlier Than Vaginal Intercourse." USATODAY.com, August 15, 2012. http://usatoday30.usatoday.com/news/health/story/2012-08-16/cdc-oral-sex/57079768/1.

Young, Saundra. "Teens Having Sex: Numbers Staying Steady." *The Chart,* June 2, 2010. http://thechart.blogs.cnn.com/2010/06/02/teens-having-sex-numbers-staying-steady/.

Chapter 14

KidsHealth. "Taking Your Child to a Therapist." September, 2010. http://kidshealth.org/parent/positive/family/finding_therapist.html#.

Thompson Jr., Dennis. "When Children Need Therapy." *Everyday Health*, July 14, 2012. www.everydayhealth.com/emotional-health/when-children-need-therapy.aspx.

Chapter 15

Dolan, Mairead. "Psychopathic Personality in Young People." *Advances in Psychiatric Treatment*. 10 (2004): 466-473. http://apt.rcpsych.org/content/10/6/466.full.

Hare, Robert D. *Hare Psychopathy Checklist-Revised: 2nd Edition*. 2003. Multi-Health Systems.

Kahn, Jennifer. "Can You Call a 9-Year-Old A Psychopath?" *The New York Times*, May 13, 2012. www.nytimes.com/2012/05/13/magazine/can-you-call-a-9-year-old-a-psychopath.html?pagewanted=all.

Lilleinfeld, Scott O. and Hal Arkowitz. "What Psychopath Means: It Is Not Quite What You May Think." *Scientific American*, November 28, 2007. www.scientificamerican.com/article.cfm?id= what-psychopath-means.

Maxted, Anna. "Is Your Child a Psychopath? It's More Common than You Think - and You Can Spot the Danger Signs as Young as Three." MailOnline.com, June 6, 2012. www.dailymail.co.uk/femail/article-2155489/Is-child-psychopath-Its-common-think-spot-danger-signs-young-three.html.

McDonald, Renee, Mary Catherine Dodson, David Rosenfield, and Ernest N. Jouriles. "Effects of a Parenting Intervention on Features of Psychopathy in Children." *Journal of Abnormal Child Psychology*, 39.7 (2011): 1013-1023.

Mustich, Emma. "Nine Year Old Psychopath: Dr. Alan Ravitz on How to Diagnose Children as Psychopaths." *The Huffington Post*, May 15, 2012. www.huffingtonpost.com/2012/05/15/diagnosing-psychopath_n_1516167.html.

Stenson, Jacqueline. "Destined as a Psychopath? Experts Seek Clues." NBCNews.com, April 20, 2009. www.msnbc.msn.com/id/30267075/ns/health-mental_health/t/destined-psychopath-experts-seek-clues/#.UHJKcY64JHg.

Chapter 16

"24 Countries Have Banned All Spanking." UPI.com, August 10, 2010. www.upi.com/Health_News/ 2010/08/10/24-countries-have-banned-all-spanking/UPI-13381281421948/.

Boyse, Kyla. "Eating Disorders: What Families Need to Know." University of Michigan Health System, October, 2010. www.med.umich.edu/yourchild/topics/eatdis.htm.

Childhelp. "National Child Abuse Statistics." www.childhelp.org/pages/statistics.

"Children Who Get Physical Punishment Tend Toward Aggression: Survey." *The Huffington Post*, February 6, 2012. www.huffingtonpost.ca/2012/02/06/children-physical-punishment-study_n_1258351.html.

Hunt, Jan. "Ten Reasons Not to Hit Your Kids." The National Child Project. www.naturalchild.org/jan_hunt/tenreasons.html.

KidsHealth. "Eating Disorders." 2011. www.kidshealth.org/parent/emotions/feelings/eating_disorders.html.

Chapter 17

Kubler-Ross, Elisabeth and David Kessler. "The Five Stages of Grief." Grief.com. http://grief.com/the-five-stages-of-grief/.